D1465486

JNTY COUNCIL
AWN

2024

03803801

ROTATION
PLAN

# AEC REGENT V

## STEWART J. BROWN

Ian Allan
PUBLISHING

# Contents

Front cover: **Aberdeen's impressive main thoroughfare, Union Street, with a 1959 Metro-Cammell-bodied Regent V against a backdrop of buildings which illustrate why Aberdeen is known as the Granite City. Aberdeen Corporation was the number two customer for Regent Vs in Scotland, with 30. The bus is followed by an Austin Cambridge A55. The last of Aberdeen's Regent Vs were withdrawn by successor Grampian Regional Transport in 1976.** Jim Thomson

Back cover (upper): **One of the first big orders for the D-series Regent V came from Glasgow Corporation but called for a non-standard specification that included a Gardner 6LW engine, a preselector gearbox and a plainer grille. There were 75 of these buses, delivered in 1955/6, with 61-seat bodies by Weymann (25) and Alexander (50)** Jim Thomson

Back cover (lower): **Since 1958 South Wales Transport had standardised on 30ft-long Regent Vs, but in 1965 switched to short models with 64-seat Willowbrook bodies. There were 21 that year, followed by a further 18 in 1966/7.** R. L. Wilson / Online Transport Archive

Previous page: **Western Welsh received its last Regent Vs in 1963 with the delivery of ten 65-seat Northern Counties-bodied 2MD3RA chassis. Similar buses were supplied to sister company Rhondda between 1964 and 1966.** Stewart J. Brown

First published 2011

ISBN 978 0 7110 3539 3

All rights reserved. No part of this book may be reproduced or transmitted in any form or by any means, electronic or mechanical, including photocopying, recording or by any information storage and retrieval system, without permission from the Publisher in writing.

© Stewart J. Brown 2011

Published by Ian Allan Publishing

an imprint of Ian Allan Publishing Ltd, Hersham, Surrey, KT12 4RG
Printed in England by Ian Allan Printing Ltd, Hersham, Surrey, KT12 4RG

Code: 1107/B1

Distributed in the United States of America and Canada by BookMasters Distribution Services

Visit the Ian Allan Publishing website at www.ianallanpublishing.com

**Copyright**
Illegal copying and selling of publications deprives authors, publishers and booksellers of income, without which there would be no investment in new publications. Unauthorised versions of publications are also likely to be inferior in quality and contain incorrect information. You can help by reporting copyright infringements and acts of piracy to the Publisher or the UK Copyright Service.

FSC
www.fsc.org
MIX
Paper from responsible sources
FSC® C014615

# Foreword

The AEC Regent in its various guises was one of the most successful bus chassis designs of its time. From 1929 to 1969 it was bought by operators large and small the length and breadth of Britain. It sold well in overseas markets too, the 250 Park Royal-bodied Regent Vs for Teheran constituting one of the biggest single export orders for complete double-deckers for a British bus builder.

The Mk V was the final development of the Regent, and it faced stiff competition, initially from Leyland's market-leading Titan and then from a new breed of rear-engined models, starting with the Atlantean and then the Fleetline.

I'm not old enough to remember the division of opinion between supporters of exposed radiators and of 'new look' fronts when these first appeared in large numbers in the 1950s. But the bonnet and grille designed for the Regent V were among the most attractive of the new-look fronts. The stylised AEC grille was certainly more subtle than Leyland's vertical slats — and longer-lived. It was still being used on export single-deckers right up to the end of AEC bus production in 1979 and still looked attractive 25 years after it had first appeared on a Regent V.

The Regent V had a loyal following, mostly from operators that were already running the previous Regent III model. The British Electric Traction group was a major user, some companies latterly buying Regent Vs and new-generation Atlanteans at the same time. There can be little doubt which was the more reliable in the early days of the Atlantean, and which generally the more economical, both in terms of fuel consumed and time spent on maintenance. But by the mid-1960s it was clear that the great days of the Regent were over. Between 1965 and 1969 fewer than 200 new Regent Vs entered service in Britain. And AEC, which had merged with arch-rival Leyland in 1962, did not have a rear-engined double-deck model to compete in the changing market — although the idea of an AEC-engined Bristol VRT is an intriguing might-have-been.

I am indebted to previous writers on the subject of AEC Regents, notably Alan Townsin, who has written extensively about the company and its products. Many photographers willingly made material available, and they are credited individually, although mention must be made of Mike Eyre, who provided high-quality scans of slides which provide those colour images credited to Roy Marshall and Geoffrey Morant. Thanks are due also to Alan Mills and the volunteers at the Omnibus Society library for giving me access to the society's extensive records.

*Stewart J. Brown*
Hebden Bridge
December 2010

# An honourable heritage

The initials 'AEC' stand for Associated Equipment Company. Associated with what? The London General Omnibus Co — for AEC was originally the bus-building arm of London's principal bus operator. The company was created in 1912 and at that time was based in Walthamstow. It moved across London in 1927 to a new purpose-built factory in Southall, where AEC would build bus chassis for just over 50 years.

AEC first coined the Regent name for a new generation of double-deck chassis in 1929. Compared with previous models the Regent had a low frame, and it set the standard for AEC double-deckers for the next 40 years. There was a companion single-deck model, the Regal, and the Regent and Regal respectively competed directly with models launched two years earlier by AEC's biggest rival in the bus business,

Leyland's Titan and Tiger. Indeed, the Titan's designer, John Rackham, had been recruited by AEC to develop its new models. The original Regent had a 6.1-litre petrol engine, but AEC was quick to offer its new 8.8-litre diesel engine as an option, from 1932. Such were the advantages of oil engines — as diesels were then known — that the vast majority of 1930s Regents were diesel-powered, although generally with the more compact 7.7-litre engine introduced in 1934. Diesel engines were noisier than petrol engines, but they were more durable and offered considerable benefits in terms of fuel economy.

When the London Passenger Transport Board was created in 1933 AEC became an independent company, but it continued as the major supplier of buses to LPTB and its successors until the early 1970s, primarily with

Below: There were detail changes over the years, but the basic style of AEC radiator remained constant throughout the first three decades of Regent production. This is a diesel-engined O661 in London Transport service, one of 400 with bodies built in LT's Chiswick Works in 1936/7 and forming part of the STL class. It was withdrawn in 1950, replaced by a new Regent III. The last exposed-radiator Regent Vs were built in 1960. R. E. Vincent

Regents and Routemasters but also — in what some might see as an ignominious end to a long-standing relationship — Merlins and Swifts.

Regent production came to a halt following the outbreak of war in 1939 but resumed in 1945, initially with the Regent II O661 model and then, from the end of 1946, with the improved Regent III O961. The key changes in the Regent III were a bigger and more powerful engine — a 125bhp 9.6-litre unit in place of the 108bhp 7.7-litre engine of the earlier model — and a pre-selector gearbox rather than a constant-mesh one. AEC soon made the smaller engine and crash gearbox available as an option in the O681 version of the Regent III.

AEC expanded in the late 1940s, acquiring Crossley and Maudslay in 1948, followed by bodybuilder Park Royal and the associated Charles H. Roe business in 1949. The Park Royal factory, in the district of the same name in north-west London, was just six miles from AEC's

Southall plant; Charles H. Roe was based in Leeds. The expanded group was known as Associated Commercial Vehicles.

In the late 1940s and early 1950s AEC's Regent III was Britain's top-selling bus chassis. It could be found from the North East of Scotland, with Aberdeen Corporation, to the far South West of England, with Devon General. But, most importantly, it could be found in London. The secret of the Regent III's success lay in huge orders from London Transport, which in the period 1947-54 took no fewer than 4,750 (its RT and RLH classes). Leyland supplied London Transport with Titans, and while the 2,131 RTL- and RTW-class Titan PD2s represented substantial business for the Lancashire manufacturer, in LT's postwar purchasing AECs outnumbered Leylands by more than two to one.

In the model's best year, 1950, an impressive 1,653 Regent IIIs entered service in Britain —

Above: The AEC Regent III was popular with operators throughout Britain. Western SMT operated 58, all with 53-seat lowbridge bodywork by Northern Counties. Delivered between 1947 and 1950, they served the company for around 16 years. Harry Hay

putting AEC almost level with Leyland, which in the same year delivered 1,674 Titans. Sales of all types of buses and coaches dropped significantly in the early 1950s, but in the period 1951-3 AEC led the field in double-deckers, the Regent III accounting for around 33% of deliveries and putting the company ahead of Leyland.

The Regent III had a broad customer base, and significant operators included the big municipal fleets in Glasgow, Leeds and Liverpool. The last-named had standardised on the Regent in the 1930s; indeed, in 1950 70% of Liverpool's fleet of 640 buses were Regents. The Scottish Omnibuses group of companies had 159, and the Regent III was also popular within the British Electric Traction group, users including Devon General, City of Oxford, Hebble, Rhondda, South Wales and Western Welsh. One of Britain's biggest independents, West Riding, also bought Regent IIIs, among them a small number of RT-style models. There was export business too, notably from Australia, Portugal and South Africa.

That the Regent III's success was due in part to London orders is not to detract from significant sales to operators elsewhere, but take London out of the equation, and the Regent III was quite clearly number two to Leyland's Titan.

Over the years the single-deck Regal had been developed in line with the Regent, but when the time came to update the Regal III AEC adopted a totally new approach, and for the Regal IV there was a horizontal engine located mid-wheelbase, under the floor. This was, of course, the future for single-deckers. It wasn't the future for double-deckers. AEC produced one underfloor-engined Regent IV, which had a short life as a demonstrator. Built in 1950, it was never registered so did not actually operate in revenue-earning service, although it was shown to a number of operators. It carried two different full-front rear-entrance bodies built by sister ACV companies, the first by Crossley, the second by Park Royal, the change of body perhaps pointing to a problem with the vehicle's weight. Compared with the Regent III the Regent IV was heavier, had a higher floor level and offered inferior engine access. There were no obvious benefits for operators or for passengers. Thus the replacement for the Regent III would be not the Regent IV but the Regent V.

In the early years of the 1950s vehicle weight was a growing concern. The main focus was on single-deckers, the switch from front-engined to mid-engined models, allied to an increase in vehicle length, heralding the arrival of a new

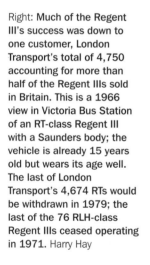

Right: Much of the Regent III's success was down to one customer, London Transport's total of 4,750 accounting for more than half of the Regent IIIs sold in Britain. This is a 1966 view in Victoria Bus Station of an RT-class Regent III with a Saunders body; the vehicle is already 15 years old but wears its age well. The last of London Transport's 4,674 RTs would be withdrawn in 1979; the last of the 76 RLH-class Regent IIIs ceased operating in 1971. Harry Hay

breed of heavy buses and coaches. With an unladen weight often approaching 8 tons a Regal IV could easily be more than a ton heavier than a Regal III. It was this concern about weight which prompted the introduction by AEC of the lighter Reliance chassis — and which also influenced double-deck developments.

A lighter-weight version of the Regent III was developed using the 7.7-litre engine and synchromesh gearbox and featuring some minor chassis changes. A demonstrator was bodied by Park Royal to gauge operator reaction, and in the spring of 1954 this featured in press advertising, in which AEC claimed that during in-service trials it had shown a 1.5mpg advantage over comparable but heavier buses. 'The new Regent leads the way to reduced operating costs', stated AEC. Some of the thinking behind the lighter-weight Regent III was to be found in the medium-weight Regent V.

As often happens in vehicle design, the Regent V was an evolution of the model it was to replace, rather than a completely new chassis. AEC stressed the evolutionary nature of its new model thus: 'The Regent Mark V double-deck bus chassis is a development of the Regent Mark III model, operated with outstanding success by numerous municipalities and company undertakings in Great Britain. Its design reflects the progressive policy of AEC in meeting the changing conditions and requirements of passenger transport operation. Improvements embodied in the Regent Mark V include a 470 cu in (7.7-litre) capacity 103bhp engine as an alternative to the well-tried 9.6-litre unit of 125bhp, both engines having a cold-air induction system.' The message in the early Regent V brochure seemed to be: 'It's new. But not too new.' AEC didn't want to frighten its customers.

At Leyland the original postwar Titan, the PD1, had used a 7.4-litre engine, the E181, and had been joined and then replaced by the larger-engined PD2, with the 9.8-litre O.600 unit. The last PD1s entered service in 1952, so from that date Leyland offered its customers just one engine, the O.600. By offering a choice of engines AEC adopted a different approach from that of its main rival. The parallel would have been Leyland's offering an upgraded version of the E181 engine in the PD2.

When the Regent V was launched the initial choice of engines lay between the new 7.7-litre AV470, in what the company described as its medium-weight MD-series chassis, and the bigger 125bhp 9.6-litre A218, carried over from the Regent III, in what would ultimately prove to be the more popular heavy-duty D-series model.

AEC's brochure stressed that the MD was designed for lightweight bodywork and that the

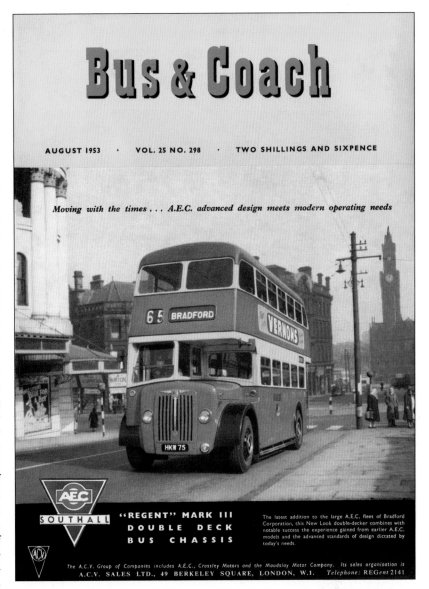

**Bus & Coach**

AUGUST 1953 · VOL. 25 NO. 298 · TWO SHILLINGS AND SIXPENCE

*Moving with the times . . . A.E.C. advanced design meets modern operating needs*

65 BRADFORD

VERNONS

HKW 75

AEC
SOUTHALL

"REGENT" MARK III
DOUBLE DECK
BUS CHASSIS

The latest addition to the large A.E.C. fleet of Bradford Corporation, this New Look double-decker combines with notable success the experience gained from earlier A.E.C. models and the advanced standards of design dictated by today's needs.

The A.C.V. Group of Companies includes A.E.C., Crossley Motors and the Maudslay Motor Company. Its sales organisation is
A.C.V. SALES LTD., 49 BERKELEY SQUARE, LONDON, W.1. *Telephone:* REGent 2141

completed bus must weigh less than 7 tons unladen. It had the same 20in wheels as the heavier-duty model but with smaller 9.00x20 tyres at the front, where the D-series used 11.00x20s. Both models had twin 9.00x20s at the rear.

An 8ft-wide MD3RV chassis weighed 4 tons 4cwt 1qr, compared with 4 tons 15cwt 1qr for an equivalent vacuum-braked D3RV. Just under half of the 11cwt weight saving came from the use of the smaller, lighter engine. According to AEC's brochure the 9.6-litre engine weighed 15cwt, while the 7.7-litre unit weighed 10½cwt. Both chassis had a 16ft 4in wheelbase, the same as on the Regent III. The gross weight of the MD was 11 tons, one ton less than the D series, which was rated at the legal maximum of 12 tons.

Like Leyland, AEC offered the choice of air or vacuum brakes, identified by the letters A or V at the end of the chassis code, and a semi-automatic or manual gearbox, identified in the chassis code by the numbers 2 or 3 respectively.

Above: The vast majority of AEC Regents with 'new look' fronts used AEC's own attractive style, first seen on the Regent V in 1954, but a small number of Regent III buyers in the early 1950s took delivery of vehicles with the Birmingham-style bonnet, including Bradford Corporation, one of whose vehicles featured in AEC advertising in 1953. This Regent was one of 40 with East Lancs bodies delivered in 1952/3. Bradford would go on to become one of the UK's top 10 Regent V customers.
Stewart J. Brown collection

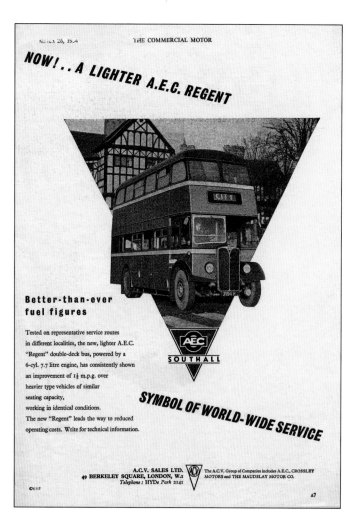

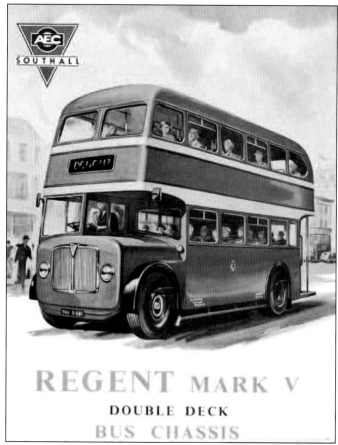

Above left: **Before the launch of the Regent V AEC produced a lightweight Regent III demonstrator with a 58-seat Park Royal body, featured in this March 1954 advertisement in** *Commercial Motor*. **It claimed fuel savings of 1½mpg over heavier vehicles. The availability of a lightweight double-decker would be central to the Regent V range in its early years. This bus was later sold to Mayne of Manchester, a long-standing Regent customer.**

Above right: **The first Regent V brochure featured an artist's impression which showed the original style of Park Royal body. Intriguingly the drawing shows, below the new-look front, an apron on which the numberplate is located — something that never appeared on a real bus.** Both Stewart J. Brown collection

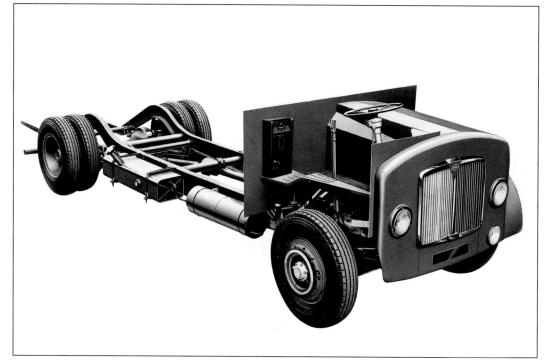

Above: **In September 1954 ACV released this image of the Regent V chassis. It shows clearly the straightforward layout of the frame, although the cab lacks the kidney-shaped instrument binnacle which was a feature of most Regent Vs. A contemporary caption claimed that 'A handsome front appearance marks the latest AEC Regent V chassis' — a statement which still holds good more than half a century later.** Ian Allan Library

Thus the MD3RV code indicated Medium weight, Double-deck, manual gearbox, Right-hand drive, Vacuum brakes.

Leyland's semi-automatic transmission was the air-operated Pneumocyclic, AEC's the electro-pneumatic Monocontrol. Both systems offered what was often described as two-pedal control, dispensing with the conventional clutch of a manual gearbox or the selector pedal of a preselector.

In promoting the new Monocontrol transmission AEC claimed that it offered 'improved performance, effortless gear changing, longer vehicle life and increased passenger comfort' and, because operators were more familiar with preselector gearboxes than semi-automatics, went on to explain: 'It is important to realise from the outset that no clutch or gear-change pedal is required with this system and that, although an epicyclic gearbox is used, this is not of preselective type; with Monocontrol Transmission the two operations of gear selection and engagement are co-ordinated as one.'

Options included an exhaust brake and automatic chassis lubrication, which was activated each time the brake pedal was pressed.

Both AEC and Leyland could supply their chassis with traditional exposed radiators or with a new-look front. Leyland's full-width bonnet and grille were developed from a structure first supplied to Midland Red in 1952. On its Regent III AEC had supplied three customers — Bradford, Kingston-upon-Hull and Devon General — with a version of what was generally known as the Birmingham front (this having been developed by Birmingham City Transport, which fitted it to Daimlers, Guys and Crossleys). And 100 Regent IIIs for Liverpool had a unique front which used the Birmingham-style grille in a full-width bonnet assembly. But for the Regent V AEC developed its own style of bonnet, which was narrower than the Leyland design, giving a slightly better view of the kerb, and featured a grille which was a stylised version of the traditional AEC radiator. To confuse the situation, a batch of late Regent IIIs for Sheffield, delivered in 1955/6, had the new Regent V grille.

New-look fronts had their detractors. One of the first road tests of a Regent V in 1956 noted: 'One wonders whether this fashion, originating

Below left: The same image as on the facing page, but with Crossley branding and no mention of the Regent V name, appeared in the September 1954 issue of *Bus & Coach*. The livery resembles that of Liverpool Corporation, which would order Crossley-bodied Regent Vs. Note that the grille is represented with additional prominent vertical bars which in effect divide it into four segments.
Gavin Booth collection

Below right: By November 1954 a different version of the original Regent V image — an offside instead of a nearside view — was encouraging readers of *Bus & Coach* to 'find out all about the NEW AEC Regent Mark V'.
Gavin Booth collection

**Crossley stands for dependability**

Ever since the early days of this century, Crossley have been building passenger vehicles noted for their sound design and construction and for their reliability under all operating conditions. Municipal authorities with some of Britain's largest fleets have long depended upon them for the maintenance of vital services.

**SEE THE LATEST CROSSLEY VEHICLES STAND 92**

COMMERCIAL MOTOR TRANSPORT EXHIBITION
EARLS COURT, LONDON.

A.C.V. SALES LTD., 49, BERKELEY SQUARE, LONDON, W.1. *Telephone: HYDe Park 2141*
A member of the A.C.V. Group of Companies which includes A.E.C., Crossley Motors, and the Maudslay Motor Co.

**Find out all about the NEW**

CITY CENTRE

**A.E.C.**

**REGENT**
MARK V

**The lighter double-decker**

A.C.V. SALES LTD.,
49 BERKELEY SQUARE, LONDON, W.1
*Telephone: HYDe Park 2141*
A member of the A.C.V. Group of Companies
which includes A.E.C., Crossley Motors,
and the Maudslay Motor Co.

AEC
SOUTHALL

from Birmingham, is a good thing or not. It is heavier, more expensive and limits engine accessibility; without the traditional radiator, most manufacturers did not know what shapes to cut into the expanse of front tin-work.

By incorporating a standard grille, the AEC attempt is, however, among those that are more pleasing, though a windscreen flush with the front panel would have been less wasteful of space, besides looking better.'

Right: The cover of *Bus & Coach* in January 1958 featured an advert by ACV's bodybuilding arm, which comprised Park Royal Vehicles, Roe and Crossley, promoted collectively as the PRV Group Body Sales Division. Unsurprisingly it featured a vehicle based on an ACV Group chassis. But this Roe-bodied Sheffield bus, which looks like a Regent V, is in fact one of a large batch of Regent IIIs supplied to the steel city in 1955/6. They were the only Regent IIIs fitted with Regent V-style new-look fronts. The Hillman Minx convertible is a nice touch.
Stewart J. Brown collection

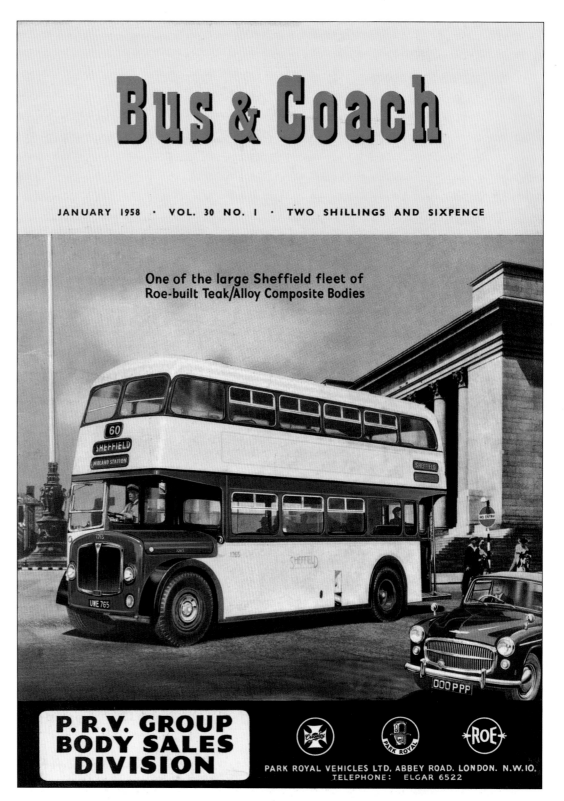

# Bus & Coach

JANUARY 1958 · VOL. 30 NO. 1 · TWO SHILLINGS AND SIXPENCE

One of the large Sheffield fleet of Roe-built Teak/Alloy Composite Bodies

**P.R.V. GROUP BODY SALES DIVISION**

PARK ROYAL VEHICLES LTD. ABBEY ROAD. LONDON. N.W.10.
TELEPHONE: ELGAR 6522

Left: This Sheffield Regent III with new-look front and Weymann Orion body is virtually indistinguishable from a Regent V. It was one of 36 similar buses on 9613S chassis with A218 9.6-litre engines and manual gearboxes. Stewart J. Brown

Left: The very first Regent V, chassis number MD3RV001, was a 1954 demonstrator with 65-seat Park Royal body. Exhibited at that year's Commercial Motor Show in London's Earl's Court, in a blue and cream livery, it is seen here on loan to Glasgow Corporation, which did order Regent Vs, albeit not to the MD-series specification. Jim Thomson

# Building on Success

The first Regent V model was the MD3RV, powered by the AV470 engine and with vacuum brakes and a synchromesh gearbox. Two chassis were completed in 1954 and bodied by sister ACV company Park Royal as 61-seaters. Both were at that year's Commercial Motor Show in London's Earl's Court. The first, originally badged as a Crossley, was used as a demonstrator by AEC, later being sold to OK Motor Services of Bishop Auckland. The second went to Walsall Corporation, an operator always ready to try new designs. The MD3RV reflected positive reaction to AEC's lightweight Regent III of late 1953, and the demonstrator had an unladen weight of just under 6½ tons — well below the 7-ton maximum set by the company.

A further 20 medium-weight chassis entered service in 1955, all Weymann-bodied buses for BET subsidiary South Wales Transport. The order was divided equally between highbridge 59-seaters and lowbridge 56-seaters.

The first big orders for the Regent V came for the heavier D-series model from two of Britain's biggest municipal fleets, both of which were replacing their tramway systems. And both ordered vehicles which were not quite standard products. Glasgow Corporation placed an order for 75, not too surprising, as they followed 265 Regent IIIs delivered between 1948 and 1951, these making up just over half of Glasgow's intake of new motor buses in that period. But what was surprising was the choice of Gardner's 6LW engine — and of a preselector gearbox, rather than the new Monocontrol semi-automatic. These were designated D2RV6G models, and had bodywork by Weymann, on 26,

Right: **The original Regent V demonstrator of 1954 was sold to OK Motor Services of Bishop Auckland. The Park Royal body of this period was particularly well-proportioned and was nicely matched to the new-look front which had been developed for the Regent V.** Harry Hay

Above: Only one other Regent V entered service in 1954, and this had the same style of Park Royal body as the demonstrator. It was delivered to Walsall Corporation. Note the sliding cab door, which at the time was relatively uncommon outside London. Roy Marshall

Left: One of the first big orders for the heavy-duty D-series Regent V came from Glasgow Corporation but called for a non-standard specification that included a Gardner 6LW engine, a preselector gearbox and a plainer grille than the AEC standard. There were 75 of these buses, chassis type D2RV6G, delivered in 1955/6, with identical 61-seat bodies built by Weymann on 25 and Alexander on the remaining 50. Jim Thomson

Right: Aberdeen Corporation specified Glasgow-style grilles on its first five Regent Vs, delivered in 1955, and these also had Gardner engines. This provided standardisation with the fleet's Daimler CVG6s, one of which is seen alongside the Regent. Sister ACV company Crossley built the 62-seat bodywork. All subsequent Aberdeen Regents had the standard AEC grille. *Harry Hay*

or by Alexander on Weymann frames (to the same design) on the remaining 49. They also featured a non-standard radiator grille — a pressed metal panel with vertical slats. This was cheaper to make and cheaper to maintain; for example, when a repaint was due, there was no polished metal grille surround to be masked. Five similar Gardner-engined chassis, but with Crossley bodies, were supplied to Aberdeen Corporation at the same time. These were Aberdeen's first Regent Vs and had the Glasgow-style grille, although subsequent buses for Aberdeen would feature the standard grille. The 6LW engine was less powerful than the AEC 9.6 (112bhp against 125bhp) and benefited from Gardner's reputation for fuel economy.

Fuel economy for the MD-series bus that was road-tested by *Passenger Transport* in 1956 was an impressive 10.75mpg fully laden. When tested with four stops a mile, to replicate regular service, the figure dropped to 10.15mpg, and in what was described as 'top gear cruising' the figure was an amazing 14.21mpg.

The other large order came from Liverpool, for 67 Regent Vs with manual gearboxes, and these deviated from the standard specification in having Glasgow-style grilles. They had Crossley bodies (but of a different design from Aberdeen's, with four rather than five bays) and

entered service in 1955/6, as did Glasgow's buses. Liverpool's initial 67-vehicle order was followed by further orders for 100 chassis with Metro-Cammell Orion bodies, but of four-bay construction rather than the standard five-bay. Delivery of these buses was spread over four years, the first arriving in 1956, the last in 1959. The protracted delivery was caused by 30 of the vehicles' being completed by the Corporation at its Edge Lane works, which, after building 15 in 1957, turned out the remainder in small numbers, just two taking to the road in 1958; the last 13 entered service in the autumn of 1959. All 167 of Liverpool's Regent Vs had Glasgow-style grilles. The later vehicles also had a built-up section on the top of the front nearside wing, to accommodate the sidelight. This was a safety feature, making the light more easily visible than when it was fitted in the normal position on the front bulkhead, under the nearside window; at this time few drivers used their headlights in urban areas at night, so sidelights were of more importance then than now. In 1958 Liverpool claimed fuel consumption of 9.4mpg for its Regent Vs.

The Gardner-engined Regent V had got off to a good start, Aberdeen and Glasgow being joined in 1956 by Rochdale Corporation, which ordered 40 with Weymann bodies. These followed the operator's first large batch of Gardner-engined buses, 30 Daimler CVG6s delivered in 1953/4, which had in turn followed 55 Regent IIIs delivered in the period 1947-51. The Rochdale buses had air brakes, and the first 30 had preselector gearboxes, like those for Glasgow; the last 10 had Monocontrol transmission.

Thus at the end of 1956 there were 120 Gardner-engined Regent Vs in service, in Glasgow, Rochdale and Aberdeen, compared with almost 300 of the AV470-powered MD-series, and just under 200 of the 9.6-litre-engined D-series. But that was it for the Gardner option. Rochdale's were the last: 120 was the total, made up of 80 D2RV6G and 40 D2RA6G models. AEC did advertise availability of Gardner's five-cylinder 5LW 7-litre engine, which a few double-deck operators were specifying in the mid-1950s, mainly in Guy and Bristol chassis, but none was built.

The success of the MD-series model was due in part to the BET group, which in 1956 took almost 150, this figure representing just over half of that year's MD deliveries. Most of these went to fleets in the South of England and South Wales — City of Oxford (17), Devon General (30), Maidstone & District (22), Rhondda (27), South Wales (21) and Western Welsh (15), plus 15 for East Yorkshire. BET companies had

considerable flexibility in body ordering, and bodies were supplied by Metro-Cammell, Park Royal, Weymann and Willowbrook. City of Oxford, East Yorkshire and Rhondda specified exposed radiators. The 22 for Maidstone & District would be that company's only new Regent Vs and had a mix of lowbridge and highbridge Park Royal bodies. East Yorkshire's buses had 56-seat highbridge Willowbrook bodies with the characteristic inward cant of the upper-deck pillars to enable buses to pass through the mediæval North Bar in the market town of Beverley.

Alongside its 15 MD-series Regents Western Welsh took eight D-series models. Hebble Motor Services also specified the heavy-duty model, taking two for its hilly territory. All of Hebble's postwar double-deckers to this point had been Regent IIIs.

A 30ft-long Regent, initially type LD2RA with Monocontrol transmission, was introduced in 1956 in response to new regulations which allowed a two-axle double-decker to be built to this length — previously only single-deckers could be 30ft long. Compared with the D2RA, the wheelbase was extended from 16ft 4in to 18ft 7in, and the front springs were revised, being increased in width from 3½in to 4in. The front frame was wider too. It also had bigger tyres, 11.00x20 on the front and 10.00x20 on

Left: The first order for standard D3RV chassis with AEC engines was placed by Liverpool, which took 67 with Crossley 58-seat bodies in 1955/6. The Liverpool grille was slightly different from that supplied to Glasgow and Aberdeen, lacking space at the top for the AEC badge and at the bottom for the Regent name. This is a 1960s view, the bus being in the final version of Liverpool Corporation's livery with cream window surrounds and the city crest and fleetname on the upper-deck side panels. Liverpool and Aberdeen were the only operators of Regent Vs with Crossley bodies. Omnicolour

Right: The Gardner-engined Regent had a short production life, which came to an end after 40 were delivered to Rochdale Corporation in 1956. They had nicely proportioned Weymann 61-seat bodies and when new wore this traditional style of livery, which dated back to 1937; they were later painted all-over cream with a band of blue relief. Rochdale's buses were the only Gardner-engined Regent Vs to be supplied with AEC's standard new-look front. They were also the only Gardner-engined Regent Vs for an English operator. All passed to SELNEC PTE in 1969. Roy Marshall

the rear. The gross weight was increased to 14 tons. There was no vacuum-braked version of the 30ft model, and it was available only at the maximum width of 8ft, while the shorter-wheelbase model continued to be available in a 7ft 6in-wide version, the pre-1950 maximum which was still favoured by some operators.

Two 30ft Regents were delivered in 1956, one to Cottrell of Mitcheldean, the other to Western Welsh. Both of the long-wheelbase Regents had 73-seat bodies by Park Royal, the Western Welsh bus having a removable glass-fibre roof, and both were exhibited at that year's Commercial Motor Show. One of the leaflets produced by AEC in July 1956 to promote the new longer model featured Crossley branding, to support the Cottrell's bus which was displayed on the Crossley stand at the Show. It switched from being a Crossley to becoming an AEC before entering service. The only Regent V actually delivered with a Crossley badge was a standard 27ft-long model for Darwen Corporation in 1957. That operator's only Regent, it followed 10 Crossley DD42s. Darwen's double-deckers were generally Leyland Titans.

The medium-weight Regent attracted a number of municipal operators, and in 1956 these were Bedwas & Machen, Doncaster, Great Yarmouth, Hartlepool, Leeds, Newcastle and West Bridgford. Leeds opted for the MD2RA model, which had Monocontrol transmission and air brakes; all of the others went for the more common MD3RV, which had the

synchromesh gearbox and vacuum brakes. In fact the only buyers of the medium-weight chassis with semi-automatic transmission were Leeds (which took 150 between 1956 and 1958) and Aberdeen (25 between 1957 and 1959). All other MD-series chassis had manual gearboxes. There was, incidentally, no vacuum-braked version of the medium-weight MD with Monocontrol transmission, a type which would have been coded MD2RV.

Leeds and Doncaster's Regent Vs had exposed radiators. Doncaster standardised on the Regent V until 1960, by which time it was running 31, all with rear-entrance Roe bodies and exposed radiators. Great Yarmouth too would place repeat orders in 1958 and 1959, building up a total of 13 — unlucky for AEC, as Great Yarmouth then switched to Daimler and Leyland, although Swifts would appear in the fleet from 1970. All of the Great Yarmouth Regent Vs were bodied by Massey Bros of Wigan.

Bedwas & Machen, which ran only seven buses, bought five Regent Vs, the last in 1964. Its first had lowbridge bodywork by Longwell Green of Bristol; subsequent deliveries would have Massey bodies. The three newest buses passed in 1974 to the new Rhymney Valley District Council operation. Hartlepool's four Regent Vs — the operator's entire fleet — were run on its behalf by local coach operator Bee Line Roadways. The Hartlepool operation was merged with the larger West Hartlepool Corporation fleet in 1967. All of West

Bridgford's new double-deckers from 1930 had been AEC Regents, apart from a solitary wartime Daimler — and even that was an AEC-engined CWA6. West Bridgford would buy another three MD-series buses, but with Reading bodies, in 1958. These were the only Regent Vs to be bodied by the small Portsmouth-based builder.

The heavy D-series chassis with AEC engine was chosen in 1956 by four municipals — Liverpool (as already mentioned), Colchester, Eastbourne and Nottingham, the last-named

taking 30 exposed-radiator chassis that had originally been ordered as Regent IIIs. The combination of heavy-duty chassis and exposed radiator was unusual, the only others being for Huddersfield and Leeds. Colchester chose 7ft 6in-wide chassis and placed repeat orders in 1957 and 1959, but when AEC dropped the option of the narrower chassis later in 1959 Colchester then switched to Leyland, which was still willing to build 7ft 6in-wide Titans.

The seven buses for Eastbourne had East

Left: City of Oxford was one of AEC's most loyal customers. It standardised on the Regent from 1930, and took its first Mk Vs in 1956. The first three had lowbridge Park Royal bodies, seating 56. One is seen in Witney, outside the Marlborough Hotel, in 1958. Half a century later the Regents have long gone, but buses still load outside the hotel, and Barclays Bank still occupies the building in the background.
Roy Marshall

Left: Later deliveries to City of Oxford in 1956 included a further seven lowbridge Regent Vs, this time with 56-seat Weymann bodies. The first 33 Regent Vs for the company had exposed radiators. Roy Marshall

Lancs bodies, and repeat orders for similar buses were placed in the period 1961-3, bringing to 22 the number running in the town. Subsequent double-deck orders went to Leyland. The 1961 buses were delivered in a mainly cream livery (which later became the fleet standard) and had translucent roof panels and full-drop opening windows on the upper deck. The aim was to offer something akin to the experience of riding on an open-top bus but in a vehicle suitable for all-weather service. The windows could be locked shut by the conductor in bad weather. Above the full-drop section was a conventional hopper-type opening window.

In 1956 AEC built a second MD2RA demonstrator with a Park Royal body, which wore a blue and cream livery and was demonstrated initially to Birmingham City Transport. It was sold in 1958 to King Alfred of Winchester. AEC's last Regent V demonstrator, it was King Alfred's first AEC. It differed from the 1954 demonstrator in having air brakes and a semi-automatic gearbox. King Alfred did not buy any more Regents but did return to AEC for Bridgemasters and Renowns. That there were only two Regent V demonstrators compares with an incredible six for the Bridgemaster — perhaps indicative of ACV's desire to promote sales of its complete integral model over the sale of chassis — and two for the Renown which replaced it.

AEC was quick to secure export sales for the new Regent. The first, an order for 30, came in 1956 from Johannesburg Municipal Transport in South Africa. Johannesburg had been buying Regents since the 1930s, and by 1959 follow-on orders would take the JMT Regent V fleet to 110

buses, all with locally built bodywork by Bus Bodies (South Africa). The JMT buses had a longer wheelbase, 17ft 6in, which was available for export models, and were 29ft 6in-long 69-seaters able to carry up to 16 standees. They were also 2.5m (8ft 2½in) wide — a dimension not legal in Britain until 1961. They were fitted with the optional export 11.3-litre engine, rated at 150bhp, to cope with the city's high altitude, almost 6,000ft above sea level. Fuel economy averaged 6.4mpg. The chassis in the original order cost £3,237 each.

The first left-hand-drive Regent Vs went to Lisbon in 1957, fulfilling an initial order for 28 buses with rear-entrance Weymann bodies. Teheran followed in 1958 with 250 Park Royal-bodied buses, with the 11.3-litre engine as supplied to Johannesburg. This was the biggest single order for the Regent V, worth £2.5 million. They were Teheran's first double-deckers, and ACV claimed this as the biggest-ever export order for complete double-deck buses. The buses were shipped to the port of Khorramshahr and then driven in convoys of around 15 at a time to their destination — a five-day journey over some 660 miles of indifferent roads.

In 1957 BET still favoured the MD version of the Regent, repeat deliveries totalling 51 vehicles to City of Oxford (16), Devon General (13), East Yorkshire (two) and South Wales Transport (20). Only five D-series buses went to BET — another three for Hebble and two for East Yorkshire. East Yorkshire's two 1957 buses were its last Regents. They were also the first 30ft-long Regents for a BET company and had Roe bodies with, as on most East Yorkshire double-deckers, the 'Beverley Bar' roof profile.

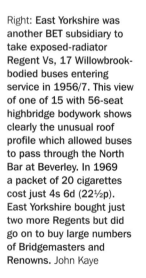

Right: East Yorkshire was another BET subsidiary to take exposed-radiator Regent Vs, 17 Willowbrook-bodied buses entering service in 1956/7. This view of one of 15 with 56-seat highbridge bodywork shows clearly the unusual roof profile which allowed buses to pass through the North Bar at Beverley. In 1969 a packet of 20 cigarettes cost just 4s 6d (22½p). East Yorkshire bought just two more Regents but did go on to buy large numbers of Bridgemasters and Renowns. John Kaye

Left: The biggest early order for Regent Vs came from Leeds City Transport, which in 1956 took 80 with 60-seat Roe bodies. This one is seen in the city's Central Bus Station soon after entering service. It might be new, but it certainly didn't look modern; Leeds specified exposed radiators on its Regents until 1960, when AEC ceased to offer the traditional radiator. Locating the numberplate below the windscreen protected it from damage in minor accidents. Like other large municipals Leeds sourced its vehicles from a number of manufacturers, as demonstrated by the Leyland Titans in the background and a Daimler CVG6 just visible at the next platform on the right of the photograph. Roy Marshall

Although East Yorkshire took no more Regents AEC continued as a supplier of double-deckers to the company until 1966, 50 Bridgemasters being followed by 34 Renowns.

There were also repeat MD orders from Aberdeen, Leeds and Newcastle corporations, while new business came from Grimsby-Cleethorpes, Morecambe & Heysham and St Helens. Aberdeen was not totally enamoured of the MD2RA, and although it placed repeat orders in 1958 and 1959 it quickly fitted Gardner 6LW engines to the last five — and then, instead of continuing to divide its orders between AEC and Daimler, standardised on the latter's CVG6, taking no more Regents; however, Aberdeen's five re-engined Regents did not last any longer than those which retained their AV470 engines, all typically running for 17 years. The five Massey-bodied buses for Morecambe & Heysham were that operator's last Regents. When they entered service Morecambe & Heysham was one of the very few operators still running petrol-engined double-deckers — prewar Regents which were returning just 3.8mpg. Its next double-deckers would be Leyland Titans.

All 40 of Newcastle's Regent Vs, delivered in two batches in 1956 and 1957, had Park Royal bodies — 30 highbridge and 10 lowbridge. As at Morecambe, they were the last for the city. Subsequent new buses for Newcastle would be supplied by Leyland, and most of these would be Atlanteans.

The Grimsby & Cleethorpes Transport Joint Committee was the newly united operation of the previously separate Grimsby and Cleethorpes corporation fleets. The Regent Vs delivered in 1957 were its first new buses and marked a continuation of Grimsby's policy of purchasing AECs. These would be Grimsby-Cleethorpes' only lightweight Regent Vs; it subsequently bought one batch of AEC Bridgemasters and then a batch of D-series Regents.

New municipal customers for D-series Regents in 1957 were Darwen (with the aforementioned Crossley-badged bus), Douglas, Ipswich and Sheffield. Ipswich had started running diesel buses as recently as 1950 (previously running only trolleybuses) and had built up a fleet of 16 Regent IIIs and eight Regal IVs when it started buying Regent Vs. The only additions to the Ipswich fleet over the next nine years were Regent Vs, to give Ipswich a total of 44, all air-braked buses with Monocontrol transmissions. The Douglas Regent Vs were that fleet's first new double-deckers since 1949. All subsequent double-deckers for Douglas would be Regent Vs. Sheffield's initial order was for 40 with Weymann Orion bodywork.

Rochdale added a further 11 D-series Regent Vs to its fleet in 1957, but this time they were standard D2RA models with AEC rather than Gardner engines. The first 10 were fitted with the standard Monocontrol semi-automatic gearbox, but the 11th had the optional fully automatic system, clumsily described by AEC as Automonocontrol — which six-syllable name, unsurprisingly, did not catch on. Four more followed in 1959. After that Rochdale's double-deckers would be Daimler Fleetlines, although the undertaking did continue to support AEC, taking small numbers of Reliances and Swifts in the 1960s.

Right: You can almost smell the paint on this brand-new Western Welsh Regent V, photographed before delivery in 1956. Fitted with a 61-seat highbridge body by Park Royal, it was one of a batch of 15 on MD3RV chassis. Geoffrey Morant

Right: Western Welsh also took eight lowbridge Park Royal-bodied Regent Vs in 1956, but on D3RV chassis. By the time this one was photographed in 1967 the company's buses were painted in unrelieved red and bore a more modern style of fleetname.
Geoffrey Morant

Top: The first Regent Vs for Hebble were two with Weymann lowbridge bodies, which entered service in 1956. This photograph was taken in 1968, by which time this bus had acquired more-modern front mudguards with curved lower edges. These were Hebble's only lowbridge Regent Vs. *Roger Holmes*

Above right and left: In 1956 Maidstone & District took 22 Park Royal-bodied Regent Vs, these comprising 14 highbridge and eight lowbridge examples. The highbridge buses seated 59, the lowbridge versions 56. A highbridge Regent is seen leaving Maidstone for Hastings (left), while the lowbridge bus is climbing out of Tunbridge Wells on its way to Hawkhurst (right). *Roy Marshall (both)*

Right and below: **Nottingham received 30 D3RV Regent Vs in 1955/6, in place of a deferred order for Regent IIIs. They had 61-seat Park Royal bodies. When new they carried a livery of green with cream relief bands (right). They were later repainted in a brighter livery, as shown by a bus which was almost 20 years old when it was photographed in Old Market Square (below), indicative of the long life achieved by some Regent Vs. Exposed-radiator D-series Regents were unusual; this was the biggest fleet, the only others being at Huddersfield and Leeds.**
Omnicolour, Stewart J. Brown

Left: This Doncaster Corporation bus looks more like a vehicle from the 1940s than the 1950s thanks to its narrow width (7ft 6in) and exposed radiator. It was one of 14 Regent V MD3RV models delivered in 1955/6, all with Roe 62-seat bodies. This is a 1973 view, and the 17-year-old bus is a credit to its operator.
Roger Holmes

Left: The first Regent V for Bedwas & Machen Urban District Council had an unusual lowbridge body by Longwell Green, based in the Bristol suburb of that name. The conservatively styled body and exposed radiator give this 1956 bus an old-fashioned look. Bedwas & Machen was one of Britain's smallest municipal operators, running just eight buses. This vehicle would be withdrawn in 1968; a 12-year life was typical for Bedwas & Machen buses. The bus in the background is a 1952 Regent III with Northern Counties body. Only three Regent Vs were bodied by Longwell Green, the other two being delivered to Pontypridd in 1966. Omnicolour

Right: **Regent Vs arrived in the AEC-oriented West Bridgford fleet in 1956 with the delivery of three MD3RV chassis with 61-seat Park Royal bodies. West Bridgford — which had standardised on Regents since 1930 — would buy more Regent Vs, but not with Park Royal bodies.**
Omnicolour

Below and opposite page top: **Hartlepool Corporation had four medium-weight Regents with 63-seat Roe bodies, which were operated on the Corporation's behalf by local coach company Bee-Line Roadways. They made up the entire Hartlepool fleet from 1956 to 1967, when it was merged with that of the neighbouring West Hartlepool Corporation. With Hartlepool they were blue; after the merger they were repainted in West Hartlepool's maroon livery.**
Roy Marshall, Harry Hay

Left: Cottrell of Mitcheldean received the first 30ft-long chassis, number LD2RA347. Both short and long versions of the D-series chassis were numbered in a common series, so it followed 346 standard-wheelbase chassis. It had a 73-seat Park Royal body with platform doors. An unusual feature was the provision of a width indicator on the nearside front wing to help the driver position the vehicle in narrow roads. The nearside wing is nevertheless damaged, although whether this happened before or after the fitting of the width indicator — which looks like a short aerial — is not recorded. Roy Marshall

# REGENT MARK V

MODEL LD2RA

CHASSIS FOR 30ft. OVERALL LENGTH BODYWORK

## SPECIFICATION

The LD2RA is a development of the " Regent " V : suitable for 30 ft. overall length bodywork. The front spring base is increased to obtain the required tilt angle with the increased top deck load possible in the longer body.

**ENGINE** A.E.C. 9·6 litre, 6-cylinder, direct injection vertical oil engine, 120 mm. (4·72 in.) bore × 142 mm. (5·59 in.) stroke, developing 125 b.h.p. at 1,800 r.p.m. ; maximum torque 430 lb. ft. at 1,000 r.p.m.

**TRANSMISSION** " Monocontrol Transmission " incorporating a fluid flywheel of latest design with bellows gland at the output shaft, and an electro-pneumatically controlled 4-speed semi-automatic, direct action, air operated epicyclic gearbox (Wilson patents) providing four forward speeds and reverse. Ratios : 1st, 4·28 : 1 ; 2nd, 2·42 : 1 ; 3rd, 1·59 : 1 ; 4th, 1·00 : 1 ; reverse, 5·98 : 1.

**PROPELLER SHAFTS** Open tubular type, fitted with Hardy Spicer needle roller bearing universal joints.

**FRONT AXLE** Forged " I " beam with integral spring pads ; stub axle diameter 2 $\frac{5}{16}$ in. Hubs mounted on taper roller bearings.

**REAR AXLE** One piece alloy steel forged axle casing ; offset underslung worm, running at 8$\frac{1}{2}$ in. centres ; fully floating axle shafts. Reduction ratios : 4$\frac{5}{8}$ : 1 ; 5$\frac{1}{5}$ : 1 ; 5$\frac{4}{5}$ : 1 ; 6$\frac{1}{4}$ : 1, and 6$\frac{3}{4}$ : 1.

**STEERING** High efficiency worm and nut ; ratio, 33 : 1or 4$\frac{3}{4}$ turns of steering wheel from lock to lock. Vertical thrust and shock is taken by a ball bearing mounted between resilient rings. Hydraulic power assisted steering is offered as an alternative at extra cost.

**BRAKE SYSTEM** Foot : compressed air operated to all wheels. Front and rear pressure systems are entirely separate and are controlled by a twin " E " valve. A compressor supplies air to two reservoirs which are charged in parallel. Hand : mechanical ratchet type to rear wheels only. " S " shaped cams and worm and wormwheel slack adjusters permit brake linings to be worn out, without use of packing pieces. Brake drums 15$\frac{1}{2}$ in. diameter, brake linings, $\frac{3}{4}$ in. thick by 4$\frac{3}{4}$ in. wide front and 7$\frac{3}{4}$ in. wide rear.

**SUSPENSION** Four reversed camber semi-elliptic leaf springs, 4 in. wide, 50 in. long front and 62 in. long rear. Resilient bump pads fitted to front and rear axles.

**FRAME** Alloy steel section side and crossmembers. Maximum frame section : $\frac{5}{16}$ in. thick, with 3$\frac{1}{2}$ in. wide flanges, 11$\frac{1}{2}$ in. deep.

**FUEL TANK** 35 Imperial gallon capacity, welded steel type. A magnetic contents gauge and a quick release filler cap are provided.

**WHEELS AND TYRES** 11·00—20, 14-ply rating single front and 10·00-20, 12-ply rating twin rear tyres.

**ELECTRICAL EQUIPMENT** 24-volt lighting and starting equipment, 7 in. diameter dynamo and axial type starter motor. Lead acid batteries of 185 or 192 ampere hour capacity.

**INSTRUMENTS AND ACCESSORIES** An instrument panel incorporating a speedometer, air pressure gauge, oil pressure gauge, coolant temperature gauge, ammeter and rheostatic switch for indirect panel lighting. A horn push, trafficator and dip switch are on an arm extending from the instrument panel.

**LOAD RATING** The chassis is sprung for weights of 5$\frac{1}{2}$ tons on the front and 8 tons on the rear axle.

**ALTERNATIVE SPECIFICATION** Single dry plate clutch and 4-speed synchromesh gearbox. Chassis with AV470 and 9·6 litre engines are also available to suit 27 ft. overall length bodies.

A.C.V. SALES LIMITED
AN A.C.V. COMPANY
49, BERKELEY SQUARE, LONDON, W.1
Telephone : HYDe Park 2141
Telegrams : " ACVESAL PHONE LONDON "

P.R.V. GROUP BODY SALES DIVISION.
PARK ROYAL VEHICLES LTD.
ABBEY ROAD, PARK ROYAL, LONDON, N.W.10.
TELEPHONE: ELGAR 6522
East Yorkshire Motor Services Limited 'Beverley Bar' type 30'-0" long double decker built by Roe. These are the first 30'-0' double deckers to be operated by this company.
THE SELLING ORGANISATION FOR
CROSSLEY MOTORS LTD.
PARK ROYAL VEHICLES LTD.
CHARLES H. ROE LTD.
STOCKPORT
LONDON
LEEDS

Annual Extra Number
Bus & Coach
THE INDUSTRY TO-DAY AND TO-MORROW
23 NOVEMBER 1957 · VOL. 29 NO. 12 · TWO SHILLINGS AND SIXPENCE
Bus builders for the world
On rough roads or made roads—on long, tough inter-city routes or heavy stop-and-go town services, A.E.C. buses may be seen working in practically every country where there are road transport facilities. Operators choose A.E.C.'s and keep on choosing them for their long, economical and trouble-free service.
Contracts for A.E.C. buses include:
WEST BENGAL 140
NEW ZEALAND (Wellington) 67
PORTUGAL 154
IRAQ (Baghdad) 35
HOLLAND (Amsterdam) 45
UGANDA 24
NEW SOUTH WALES (Sydney) 125
This picture shows one of the 50 new A.E.C. "Regent" Mark V.'s on service in Johannesburg.
AEC SOUTHALL
A.C.V. SALES LTD., 49 BERKELEY SQUARE, LONDON, W.1
The A.C.V. Group of Companies includes A.E.C. and THE MAUDSLAY MOTOR COMPANY

**Above left: Published in July 1956 to coincide with a revision to the Construction & Use Regulations permitting 30ft-long buses, this brochure for the new LD2RA version of the Regent V promoted it as a Crossley. This supported the presence of the first 30-footer on the Crossley stand at that year's Commercial Motor Show at Earl's Court in September.** Stewart J. Brown collection

**Above: The BET group's first 30ft Regent Vs were two Roe-bodied buses delivered to East Yorkshire in 1957. They had 'Beverley Bar' roofs, profiled to allow buses to pass through the ancient structure in that town. This is a 1958 advertisement. They were East Yorkshire's last Regents.** Gavin Booth collection

**Left: A Johannesburg Regent V was used for a 1957 'Bus builders for the world' advertisement by ACV Sales, which boldly claimed that 'AEC buses may be seen working in practically every country where there are road transport facilities'.** Stewart J. Brown collection

Right: The first export order for the Regent V was received from Johannesburg Municipal Transport, which in 1956 took delivery of 30 D2RA models with 11.6-litre engines and 69-seat bodies by Bus Bodies (South Africa). A script 'Regent' badge is carried on the grille, while the front bumper was a feature on many export Regent Vs. Repeat orders would take the Johannesburg Regent V fleet to 110 by 1959. Stewart J. Brown

Below: Mayne of Manchester was among the early buyers of the 30ft-long Regent V, three LD3RA models entering service on the company's route between Manchester and Droylsden in the summer of 1957. They had 73-seat Park Royal bodies. This one is seen in Manchester city centre in 1973, still smart despite being 16 years old. Mayne was at this time the only independent operator running a regular service in the city. Stewart J. Brown

Above: The only 30ft-long
Regent Vs with rear-
entrance lowbridge
bodywork were two supplied
to Barton Transport in 1957.
The 67-seat bodies were by
Northern Counties and were
similar to those being
supplied to the Scottish Bus
Group on Leyland Titan PD3
chassis. Roy Marshall

Right: The first Regent Vs
for Grimsby-Cleethorpes
Transport were seven
medium-weight models with
63-seat Park Royal bodies.
These were delivered in
1957, the year the two
councils merged their
bus operations. This bus
displays both towns' crests.
Roy Marshall

Left: Morecambe & Heysham Corporation was still operating prewar petrol-engined Regents when it took delivery of five Massey-bodied Regent Vs in 1957. New AECs were a rarity with municipal fleets in the North West of England, most of which supported their local manufacturer, Leyland. The Morecambe & Heysham operation was absorbed by neighbouring Lancaster when local government was reorganised in 1974. Roy Marshall

Below: After buying five Gardner-engined Regent Vs in 1955, Aberdeen switched to the AV470-engined MD2RA model, taking 25 between 1957 and 1959. The 15 delivered in 1958 had Metro-Cammell Orion bodies. The shortened front wings, an Aberdeen modification, reduced their vulnerability to minor accident damage. These buses replaced the city's last trams, which were just nine years old. Harry Hay

Right: Aberdeen's experience with the AV470 engine wasn't entirely satisfactory, and in 1963 it re-engined its last five, supplied in 1959, with Gardner 6LW engines. These buses had 66-seat Alexander bodies. To accommodate the larger engine the radiator grille had to be moved forward an inch or so, a modification just visible in this 1965 view. Harry Hay

Below: Like many AEC users, Douglas Corporation progressed from Regent IIIs to Regent Vs. Its first Mk Vs were four with 56-seat Metro-Cammell Orion bodies, delivered in 1957 and featuring an unusual triangular window below the staircase. One stands alongside a Northern Counties-bodied Regent III, one of 18 delivered in the late 1940s. Omnicolour

Left: The first heavy-duty Regent Vs for City of Oxford were 16 30ft-long LD3RA models delivered in 1957/8. The body order was divided equally between Weymann, as seen here, and Park Royal. Although the buses were 30ft long, City of Oxford specified just 65 seats, a capacity which some operators were achieving on 27ft models. A summer Sunday in 1960 shows how quiet city streets were in the days when shops were closed on Sundays. Roy Marshall

Below: The radiator of the preserved Darwen Regent V shows how the Crossley badge was fitted in the space normally occupied by the AEC name. Stewart J. Brown

Below: Only three Regent Vs carried Crossley badges, and only one retained its Crossley badge when it entered service. That bus was for Darwen Corporation and had an East Lancs body. Seen in Darwen bus station, this bus has since been preserved. Subsequent Darwen double-deckers would be Leyland Titans. Omnicolour

31

Above and right: **Lowbridge** buses were relatively uncommon in English municipal fleets. Newcastle Corporation's 40 Park Royal-bodied Regent Vs delivered in 1956/7 included 10 lowbridge examples for use on a service between the city centre and Ponteland, which passed under a low railway bridge at Kenton Bank Foot; the remaining 30 were of highbridge layout. The mixture of similar lowbridge (above) and highbridge (right) Park Royal bodies echoed deliveries to Maidstone & District and Western Welsh at around the same time, as illustrated on **page 21**. Roy Marshall (both)

Left: Liverpool had 100 VKB-registered Regent Vs with Metro-Cammell Orion bodies which had four bays rather than the standard five. Delivery started in November 1956 but was not completed until October 1959; 30 of the buses had bodywork finished by the Corporation at its Edge Lane works, and these were built in small numbers over three years. New in 1957, this bus wears the original livery used on Liverpool's Regent Vs, with bands of cream relief. Note the nearside sidelight, fitted to an extension built on to the front wing. All but five of these buses would pass to Merseyside PTE in December 1969. Omnicolour

Left: South Wales Transport was one of the first operators of the MD3RV, in 1955, and its 1957 deliveries — the company's last MD-series buses — took the number in the fleet to 61. Subsequent deliveries would be D-series chassis. This bus was one of 10 delivered in 1957 which had 61-seat Weymann Orion bodies. Glengettie tea is still sold in Wales. Omnicolour

# Medium-weight minority

Including the Gardner-engined buses, sales of Regent Vs between 1955 and 1957 were split just about evenly between the heavy-duty D and the medium-duty MD. By the end of 1957 there were just over 600 MD-series Regent Vs in service, of which around 225 were for BET subsidiaries — compared with just 16 D-series models in BET service. But that changed from 1958, sales of the AV470-engined model dropping rapidly. This can best be illustrated by comparing 1957 deliveries of just over 150 to 1958's figure of just 41, after which annual MD-series sales averaged fewer than 20 a year in the first half of the 1960s. The bulk of the 1958 sales of the MD went to two municipal fleets, Aberdeen and Leeds, each of which took 15. None went to BET companies.

Instead BET went for the 30ft-long LD3RA, in 1958 taking 74, which were shared between City of Oxford (16, its first Regents with new-look fronts), Hebble (two), Rhondda (20), South Wales (26) and Yorkshire Woollen (10). The Oxford buses had rear-entrance bodies by Weymann or Park Royal with just 65 seats and were used mainly on city services; all the other

companies switched to high-capacity 70- or 71-seat forward-entrance Orion-style bodies by Metro-Cammell or Weymann. The forward-entrance Orion was, technically, an Aurora, but that name was little used. These BET-group buses were the first forward-entrance Regent Vs.

Having taken half a dozen MD-series Regents in 1957, St Helens switched to the D-series in 1958, taking delivery of 24, the body order being split between Weymann (16) and East Lancs (eight). These completed the town's trolleybus-replacement programme and also replaced some 10-year-old Regent IIIs. St Helens divided its chassis orders between AEC and Leyland and would continue buying both Regent Vs and Titan PD2s until 1967. Most of the Regents would be heavy-duty chassis, but St Helens did revert to the MD-series model for one batch of buses in 1959.

Huddersfield was a new Regent V customer in 1958, taking eight old-fashioned-looking exposed-radiator D-series chassis with 65-seat Roe bodies. Whereas Leyland offered exposed-radiator Titans until the end of production in 1969, AEC was quick to drop the exposed-

Right: The first forward-entrance Regent Vs for BET-group companies entered service in 1958. These included 10 for Yorkshire Woollen District which had 70-seat Metro-Cammell Aurora bodies. By 1960 YWD would be running 34 buses of this style.
Geoffrey Morant

Left: In 1958 Hebble took two 30ft-long Regent Vs with forward-entrance Weymann bodies and followed these with another three in 1959, one of which is seen here in Leeds in 1963. By now Hebble was running 17 Regent Vs, the type making up the company's entire double-deck fleet; this one is setting out on the service across the Pennines to Burnley via Halifax, a 35-mile trip. This and most other Hebble services would be taken over by the Halifax Joint Omnibus Committee in 1971. R. F. Mack

radiator option, few being built after 1958. Indeed, in a 1957 brochure the company stated: 'For chassis ordered in economic quantities, models MD2RA, MD3RV, D2RA, D3RV are available … with half-front dash structure and exposed radiator.' The last exposed-radiator Regent Vs went to Leeds City Transport in 1960; clearly 14 chassis for such an important customer counted as an economic quantity. Leeds was easily the biggest user of exposed-radiator Regent Vs, with 164 in operation when the last were delivered.

A number of small operators bought Regent Vs. In the latter half of the 1950s six Yorkshire operators — Blue Ensign, Burrows, Felix, Ledgard, United Services and York Pullman — bought 15 between them. All loyally specified locally built Roe bodywork, and Blue Ensign's bus was that company's first new double-decker, and was at that time unusual for a small operator in being of forward-entrance layout. The Ledgard business was bought in 1967 by West Yorkshire Road Car, which thus became the only Tilling-group operator of Regent Vs. It acquired 10 from the Ledgard fleet, the six bought new plus four which had started life with South Wales Transport.

Three Scottish independents took Regent Vs in the 1950s, Baxter of Airdrie, Garelochhead Coach Services and Greenshields of Salsburgh all choosing medium-weight MD3RV models. Baxter generally bought Leyland Titan double-deckers and AEC Reliance single-deckers; the two Regents delivered in 1957 temporarily broke that pattern. They had lowbridge Massey bodies, as had the Greenshields bus. Garelochhead's two Regents, with Alexander

bodies, were the company's first new double-deckers.

Other independent buyers were Kearsey of Cheltenham, Osborne of Tollesbury, Mayne of Manchester (all with Park Royal bodies) and Barton Transport. The three buses for Mayne and the two for Barton were among the first production 30ft-long Regents. Barton Transport operated a distinctive fleet. Its two Regent Vs had lowbridge 67-seat Northern Counties bodies, with conventional rear entrances, albeit with platform doors. They were the only 30ft Regent Vs with lowbridge rear-entrance bodies,

Above: With 450 buses, the Teheran Omnibus Board was easily the biggest customer for the Regent V. This Park Royal-bodied bus, one of 250 supplied in 1958, is seen in service in 1973. These were the first left-hand-drive Regent Vs with new-look fronts and were of chassis type D2LA, the 'L' indicating left-hand drive. When new these buses were painted red, a livery inspired by London Transport. Julian Osborne

Right: The Teheran order was an important one for ACV, involving as it did the supply of both chassis and bodies. This 1958 Park Royal advertisement describes the order as 'another ACV Group triumph'.
Gavin Booth collection

AND NOW PERSIA!

★ PARK ROYAL bodies again selected for the MIDDLE EAST! One of the 250 73-seater double deckers for the TEHERAN OMNIBUS BOARD.
Our long export experience in world-wide markets is built in to the special design prepared for Teheran. This is the largest overseas contract ever placed with the British Passenger Vehicle Industry for complete double deckers and spares.
The bodies are mounted to the A.E.C. "Regent" Mk.V chassis making this another A.C.V. Group triumph.

P.R.V GROUP BODY SALES DIVISION
PARK ROYAL VEHICLES LTD., ABBEY ROAD, LONDON, N.W.10
TELEPHONE: ELGAR 6522

as AEC guided buyers needing a high capacity within a low overall height to the Bridgemaster.

A minor change was made to the radiator grille on the new-look front from late 1958. The original design had vertical slats; the revision saw a mesh grille being adopted. The only other change to the grille — towards the end of production, in 1966 — was the addition of individual 'AEC' letters on the lower nearside section. But by this time Regent V sales were in decline, and it is unlikely that the new lettering appeared on more than 100 home-market buses. In any event, the letters often disappeared. Another detail change, in 1959, was to the shape of the lower edge of the front wings, with the adoption of a stylish curve. This was in part to address problems of the original design interfering with the operation of automated bus-washing machines.

By 1959 there was a growing emphasis on the 30ft-long version of the Regent V, and of 86 D-series models entering service that year 73 were long models, 68 of them for BET companies. These included repeat orders from Hebble (four), South Wales (nine) and Yorkshire Woollen (15), but more interestingly there were 40 for a new Regent buyer, East Kent. East Kent had previously bought Leyland Titans and, more recently, Guy Arabs, but also ran a large fleet of AEC Reliances. Its Regent Vs had 72-seat forward-entrance full-front Park Royal bodywork and a new engine, the AV590. This was the same size as the engine it was replacing, 9.8 litres, but of a different design. It was rated at 128bhp — barely any different from the previous engine's 125bhp rating. Regent Vs with the AV590 engine were given a '2' prefix to their chassis code; the East Kent buses were thus 2LD3RA models and, like most previous BET group Regent Vs, had synchromesh gearboxes. One of these attractive vehicles was exhibited at the 1958 Commercial Motor Show.

Outwardly identical to the East Kent batch, but with Monocontrol transmission, was the Regent V supplied in 1959 to Liverpool Corporation, becoming its first (and only) 30ft-long Regent, and its first (and only) forward-entrance — as distinct from front-entrance — double-decker. It was one of three experimental high-capacity buses evaluated by the Corporation, the others being a Leyland Atlantean and an AEC Bridgemaster demonstrator that was supplied in Liverpool livery and later purchased by the Corporation. As history would show, the Atlantean was the winner, Liverpool going on to order more than 500.

The use of the 'L' prefix for long-wheelbase chassis was discontinued in 1959, so, for example, identical models delivered to Yorkshire Woollen changed from being coded 2LD3RA in 1959 to 2D3RA in 1960. And it was at this point that the 7ft 6in-wide short-wheelbase model, a minority choice, was dropped.

Bradford took delivery of 15 30ft Regents with 70-seat forward-entrance Metro-Cammell bodies in 1959 and then standardised on the type, having 120 in operation by 1964. The first 30 had Monocontrol gearboxes, but subsequent deliveries saw a switch to manual transmission. With its hilly routes, Bradford was one of relatively few operators to specify exhaust brakes, claiming their use cut expenditure on rear brakes by 17% and on front brakes by an impressive 28.5%.

Similar to the Bradford vehicles were the Metro-Cammell-bodied buses, 16 in all, delivered in 1960 to the Halifax Corporation and Joint Omnibus Committee fleets — Halifax's only Regent Vs. Meanwhile, in 1959, St Helens took a one-off 30-footer, with a forward-entrance 73-seat East Lancs body. It remained unique in the St Helens fleet, which would continue to buy open-platform rear-entrance buses for as long as it bought double-deckers.

Although the Regent was AEC's principal double-deck model in the late 1950s it wasn't the only one. Series production of Routemasters for London Transport got underway in 1959, in which year almost 200 were delivered. And then there was the low-height Bridgemaster integral, which AEC supplied in relatively small numbers from 1958, some to operators that had also bought Regent Vs, in particular BET subsidiaries

Left: Baxter's Bus Service operated a smart fleet on local services in Airdrie and Coatbridge. In the 1950s the company normally bought AEC single-deckers and Leyland double-deckers, but in 1957 it took a pair of medium-weight Regent Vs, as well as three Titans. The attractive 55-seat lowbridge bodywork was by Massey. The Baxter's business was purchased in December 1962 by Scottish Omnibuses, which continued to operate the two ex-Baxter Regents until 1974.
Iain MacGregor

Below: Two Alexander-bodied MD-series Regent Vs were delivered to Garelochhead Coach Services, in 1958 and 1959. This bus has the unusual combination of the original, vertically slatted grille and the later style of front wings with a curved leading edge. Note the company's attention to detail in the neatly painted wheels with cream rims.
Stewart J. Brown

East Yorkshire, South Wales and Western Welsh and municipal Grimsby-Cleethorpes.

Thus by 1960 AEC was offering three double-deck models — Regent V, Routemaster and Bridgemaster. Ten years earlier it had just one, the Regent III. One effect of this was that Regent V sales would never match those of the Regent III. In 1950 AEC accounted for around one-third of UK double-deck deliveries with just one model; in 1960 it held the same share of the market — after some lean years when no new buses were being delivered to London Transport — but spread across three models. The Regent V accounted for just under 10% of double-deck deliveries, compared with 20% for the rival Leyland Titan. But perhaps this didn't seem important to ACV's management, for 1960's top-selling double-decker was the Routemaster, which meant that the company still enjoyed a healthy share of the market for double-deck buses.

Despite the existence of six demonstrators, the effort expended by AEC in developing the Bridgemaster yielded just 174 sales over six years; typically more Regent Vs were sold in a single year. And the Routemaster really was a bus for London. When ACV finally did offer a Routemaster for demonstration, in 1962, it made use of London Transport's unique forward-entrance RMF1254. This seemed a shade half-hearted; it was as much ACV's finding a use for an unwanted bus as a serious attempt to convince operators outside London that the Routemaster was the bus they should be buying — a view supported by the fact that the vehicle was tried by only three operators. These were Liverpool, where it was being evaluated at the same time as the first of an order for 200 Atlanteans was entering service (and was thus clearly a non-starter), East Kent, which continued to buy Park Royal-bodied Regent Vs, and Halifax. However, ACV did manage to find one customer for the Routemaster outside London, Northern General switching from Atlanteans for 50 forward-entrance versions delivered in 1964/5.

Below and opposite top:
One of the biggest orders for Regent Vs from an independent operator came from Ledgard of Leeds, which in 1957 took six with 65-seat Roe bodies. They passed to the West Yorkshire Road Car Co with the Ledgard business in 1967. Not many buses received reversed registrations with a single letter. Roy Marshall, R. L. Wilson / Online Transport Archive

Left: A smaller Yorkshire delivery in 1957 saw two Regent Vs with lowbridge Roe bodies join the fleet of Bingley, one of three operators trading as United Services. Bingley was based in Kinsley, which was roughly midway between United Services' principal destinations of Wakefield and Doncaster. Only one other Regent V, delivered to Burrows of Wombwell in 1956, had a lowbridge Roe body. John Kaye

Above: A number of small operators bought new Regent Vs, including Kearsey of Cheltenham, which in 1957 placed in service this lowbridge Park Royal-bodied bus, seen unloading in the town's bus station in 1971.
John Aldridge

Right: Osborne of Tollesbury bought one new Regent V, a D2RA delivered in 1957, with stylish lowbridge Park Royal body fitted with platform doors. It is seen in Colchester bus station, ready to head back to its home town. Lowbridge bodywork on Regent Vs was not that common, AEC being able to offer low-height alternatives in the form of first the Bridgemaster and then the Renown.
Omnicolour

Left: Exposed-radiator Regent Vs were very much in the minority. In 1958 Huddersfield took eight D2RA models — its first Regent Vs — with Roe bodies; subsequent deliveries would have new-look fronts. Startips disinfectant offered 'a garland of flowers in a bottle', demonstrating that there's nothing new in fanciful advertising to promote utilitarian household products.
Stewart J. Brown

Below: Between 1950 and 1959 all 36 new buses purchased by Ipswich Corporation were Park Royal-bodied AECs. These included 12 Regent Vs, delivered between 1957 and 1959. More Regents would follow, but not with Park Royal bodies. R. L. Wilson / Online Transport Archive

Right: **Only three Regent Vs were bodied by Reading & Co of Portsmouth. They were MD3RV models for West Bridgford and entered service in 1958. The lowbridge bodywork seated 59 passengers. Reading bodies were generally supplied to local operators; West Bridgford's Regents marked the company's northernmost double-deck order.** Iain MacGregor

Right: **This fine photograph of a St Helens Corporation Regent V was taken at the AEC works in Southall in 1958 as the bus was on delivery from the Weymann factory in Addlestone, Surrey. It was one of 16 based on heavy-duty D3RV chassis and followed six similar buses delivered the previous year but on medium-weight MD3RV chassis. Many municipal fleets quoted not just the general manager's name as part of the legal lettering but also his qualifications. The wording on the side of this vehicle reads 'John C. Wake, M Inst T, ACIS, MIRTE, General Manager & Engineer', indicating his membership of the Institute of Transport, the Chartered Institute of Secretaries and the Institute of Mechanical Engineers.** Ian Allan Library

Above: **Also delivered to St Helens in 1958 were eight D3RV Regent Vs, with East Lancs bodywork. Most of them served the town for 13 years, much the same life as the lighter MD-series models received by the Corporation in the latter part of the 1950s.** Roy Marshall

Left: **In the late 1950s a small number of operators showed an interest in unpainted buses. They included South Wales Transport, which took this Weymann-bodied bus, the last of seven Regent Vs delivered in 1959. As this view shows, the buses could look good when new, but operational experience showed that they didn't weather well, and any thoughts of saving money (and weight) by dispensing with paint were quickly forgotten.** Harry Luff / Online Transport Archive

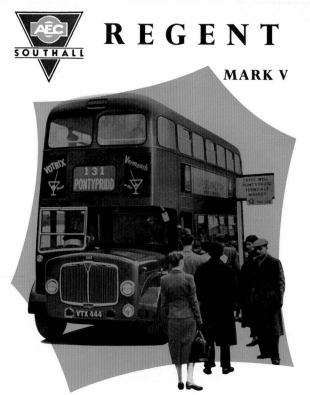

REGENT

MARK V

**AEC SOUTHALL**

**DOUBLE-DECK BUS CHASSIS**

Above: **More typical of deliveries to BET operators in South Wales is this 1958 Regent V for Rhondda, one of 20 long-wheelbase LD3RA models with 70-seat Weymann Aurora bodywork. The unrelieved red paint — it seems inappropriate to dignify the vehicle's appearance with the word 'livery' — did Rhondda's Regents no favours. Note also the mismatch in the front wings, the squared-off original on the nearside contrasting with a later replacement on the offside.** Harry Luff / Online Transport Archive

Left: **One of Rhondda's 1958 Regent Vs featured on the cover of an AEC brochure published that year.** Ian Allan Library

Left: The biggest BET-group order for Regent Vs came from East Kent, which received 40 Park Royal-bodied 30-footers in 1958/9. They had stylish full-width fronts, and later in their lives some were converted for one-man operation, as seen here in the summer of 1971. The company's first AEC Regents, they set the standard for deliveries through the 1960s. 'Camber' seems as much a warning as a destination as the bus leans towards the kerb outside Rye station. John Aldridge

Left: The only other Park Royal body to the same style as those for East Kent was a one-off for Liverpool Corporation which was noteworthy for a number of reasons, being Liverpool's last new front-engined bus, its only forward-entrance double-decker, its only Regent V with a standard AEC grille and the first bus in the fleet to be fitted with saloon heaters. New in 1959, it was an LD2RA model. Inherited by Merseyside PTE in 1969, it would be withdrawn in 1974 and subsequently preserved. Roy Marshall

Above: **Between 1956 and 1959 Colchester Corporation bought 11 Regent Vs with 61-seat Massey bodies. These were 7ft 6in wide, and when AEC dropped this width option Colchester switched its orders to Leyland, which was willing to supply 7ft 6in-wide Titans. One of the 1959 buses is seen in the town's High Street in 1964.** Roy Marshall

Right: **AEC did quite well with municipalities in East Anglia in the late 1950s, supplying Ipswich, Colchester and, as seen here, Great Yarmouth. Unlike the other two operators Great Yarmouth specified the AV470-engined MD-series chassis. There were 13 Regent Vs in the Great Yarmouth fleet, all with 58-seat Massey bodies.** Roy Marshall

Above: St Helens had just one 30ft-long Regent, which was also the operator's only forward-entrance double-decker. New in 1959, it had a 73-seat East Lancs body and was intended for use on longer services, such as that to Southport, its destination in this late-1960s view.
Roy Marshall

Left: London Transport, the biggest customer for the Regent III, did not buy any Regent Vs, choosing instead the integral AEC/Park Royal Routemaster. It took 2,760 front-engined Routemasters, the bulk delivered between 1958 and 1968. Most used the AEC AV590 engine, as fitted to the majority of D-series Regent Vs. A 1967 bus approaches Marble Arch from Edgware Road in 1983.
Stewart J. Brown

# CHAPTER 4

# Longer buses lead

By 1960 there was growing interest in maximum-capacity double-deckers, and in that year Sheffield Corporation took delivery of 46 Regent Vs, all of which were 30ft long, with rear-entrance bodies by Alexander (20) or Weymann (26). These, together with six Bridgemasters delivered at the same time, replaced the last of the city's trams. There were also 25 Roe-bodied buses for what was known as the 'B' fleet, owned jointly by Sheffield Corporation and British Railways.

Another buyer of 30ft-long Regents to replace trams was Glasgow Corporation, which in 1960 took the first of 89 buses with 72-seat forward-entrance Alexander bodies, delivery of which was spread over three years. The Regents were accompanied by 140 similar Leyland Titans. Glasgow had originally planned to have Gardner engines again, as in its 1955 buses, but AEC talked the Corporation out of that, and the vehicles had AEC's standard AV590 engine. However, like the fleet's previous Regent Vs,

they had the simplified grille. This was AEC's biggest single order for Regent Vs in the UK — beating an 80-vehicle order from Leeds in 1956 — and was the company's last double-deck fleet order from Scotland; Glasgow then switched to rear-engined Atlanteans. The Sheffield and Glasgow buses were the only 30ft Regents to be bodied by Alexander.

High-capacity Regent Vs were also used by South Wales Transport, to replace the trams on the five-mile-long Swansea & Mumbles Railway, taken over in 1958. The last of the line's huge (106-seat) 30-year-old double-deck trams ran in January 1960.

Leeds City Transport, which had been buying AV470-engined Regents, switched in 1960 to the 30ft-long 2D2RA with the AV590 engine, taking 14 — the only 30ft Regents with exposed radiators. They had Metro-Cammell Orion bodies. Leeds was at this time sharing its chassis orders between AEC, Daimler and Leyland, body orders going to Metro-Cammell and to local

Right: **In 1960 Sheffield took delivery of 71 30ft-long Regent Vs, shared between the Corporation and the Joint Omnibus Committee fleets and with bodywork by three builders — Roe, Alexander and, as on this bus, Weymann. There were 26 Weymann-bodied buses, all for the Corporation fleet. They were 2D3RA models with AV590 engines and manual gearboxes.**
Stewart J. Brown

Left: The 20 Alexander-bodied buses for Sheffield were of an unusual style with 30ft-long rear-entrance bodywork, a layout supplied to only two other operators — Glasgow and Cardiff. Despite their length they seated just 65. Roy Marshall

builder Roe. It would carry on buying Regent Vs until 1965/6 and continued to support AEC thereafter with orders for Swifts, delivered alongside Atlantean and Fleetline double-deckers. Leeds was Britain's biggest Regent V user, the final deliveries in 1966 bringing the number in service to 224. It would also become the biggest Swift operator outside London, having 120 in service by the end of 1971.

Nearby Huddersfield switched to 30ft Regents in 1960, taking two with forward-entrance East Lancs bodies, which were followed in 1961 by a further two similar buses. The last Regents for Huddersfield were six with Roe bodies in 1962; here AECs were very much in the minority, being outnumbered by the products of Leyland and Daimler, the latter becoming the town's principal supplier.

On two services passing under low bridges in Llanelli — the lowest with only 9ft clearance — South Wales had been operating Regal III single-deckers with a low roof profile, and when these

Left: The Roe-bodied Regent Vs which joined the Sheffield fleet in 1960 were 69-seaters with platform doors. There were 25. Roy Marshall

Right: The last new half-cab single-deckers to enter service in Britain, in 1963, were six Regent Vs for South Wales Transport. They had 37-seat Roe bodies and were operated on two routes in Llanelli, where a particularly low bridge precluded the use of underfloor-engined single-deckers. They would be withdrawn in 1972.
Omnicolour

became due for replacement the company was faced with the fact that an underfloor-engined bus wouldn't fit. So it came up with an ingenious solution: fit single-deck bodywork to a Regent V. Two such buses, bodied by Roe, were delivered in 1959, to be followed by six more in 1963. All were 37-seaters, and in common with most BET Regents of this period they were heavy D-series chassis in the interests of standardisation, rather than lighter MD-series models, which might have seemed a more obvious choice for single-deckers. They were just 8ft 10in high.

After buying 30ft-long Regents in 1958, City of Oxford returned in 1960 to short models and the AV470 engine, taking 15. Five, bodied by East Lancs, were rear-entrance buses of lowbridge configuration (being the last examples of either supplied to the company); the other 10 had forward-entrance bodywork by Willowbrook. Oxford would stay with AEC but thereafter bought Bridgemasters and Renowns rather than Regents; the Willowbrook-bodied Regents would be its last full-height buses until the days of the National Bus Company.

It is a measure of the waning popularity of the lightweight Regent V that the only other deliveries in 1960 were two for Doncaster (its last Regents) and one with a forward-entrance Willowbrook body for Cottrell of Mitcheldean, where it joined an early 30ft-long D-series. There were also a couple of non-PSV single-deckers, bodied by Roe, for the Coal Industry Social Welfare Organisation and Leeds City Council Welfare Services. In 1961 AEC would supply only one MD-series Regent, to Bedwas &

Machen. Two further non-PSV Regents were built in 1961, being supplied as vans to St Helens-based glass manufacturer Pilkington.

Alongside repeat business from established buyers, the 2D-series Regent picked up a few new customers in 1961. Bolton Corporation took six long-wheelbase versions, with 70-seat forward-entrance bodies by Metro-Cammell. These were the operator's first (and only) new AECs since a Q-type in 1933. In Ireland, CIE, which had standardised on the Leyland Titan PD3, took three 30ft-long Regents; these were the only Regent Vs for an Irish operator and had been ordered by the Great Northern Railway (Ireland), which had operated 29 Regent IIIs and had been absorbed by CIE in 1958. They were based in Waterford, where they replaced trains on the line to Tramore. For this duty they had space to store goods at the rear of the lower deck, which reduced the seating capacity of their CIE-built bodies to 69, compared with 74 on the operator's PD3s.

West Bridgford, with half a dozen MD-series Regents in service, switched to the heavy-duty 2D model in 1960, taking a couple of East Lancs-bodied buses. Four more would follow, two each in 1962 and 1964. West Bridgford then ordered two Renowns, its last double-deckers, for delivery in 1965, followed by three AEC Swifts, its last buses, in 1967. The 28-bus operation was taken over by Nottingham City Transport in 1968, and of the buses that passed to NCT 23 were Regents, including 12 Regent Vs.

While AEC had some success with the Regent at Nottingham and West Bridgford and with

Above: **The only new Regent Vs for Halifax were 16 delivered in 1960 and shared equally between the Corporation and Joint Omnibus Committee fleets. They were 2D3RA models and had 72-seat Metro-Cammell bodies. A lorry in the background illustrates how AEC used the same grille on both goods vehicles and buses.** Roy Marshall

Left: **In 1960 Leeds City Transport took 14 Regent Vs with Metro-Cammell Orion bodywork. These were significant in being the only 30ft-long Regent Vs to have exposed radiators, and they were the only Leeds Regent Vs not to be bodied by Roe. They were also among the last exposed-radiator Regents to enter service; subsequent buses for Leeds would have new-look fronts.** Stewart J. Brown

independent Barton Transport, elsewhere in the Midlands it fared badly. The only other Regent V customer in the region was Walsall, which had taken the second Regent V built, in 1956, and then took one batch of 10 in 1961. These were forward-entrance 72-seaters, the body order being divided equally between Metro-Cammell and Willowbrook.

A new style of Park Royal body appeared on a batch of 16 Regent Vs for East Kent in 1961. Like the company's earlier vehicles it was a forward-entrance 72-seater, but now of a style which owed something to the AEC Bridgemaster body, and featured shallow upper-deck windows and deep lower-deck windows — a feature most commonly associated with the MCW Orion. It also had a conventional half-cab. Few would have judged the new body an improvement. All subsequent Regent Vs for East Kent, up to the last in 1967, would be of generally similar design with but detail differences.

The same body was used for a solitary Regent V delivered in 1961 to British European Airways. The seating capacity was just 55, with 17 seats in the lower saloon, compared with 32 on the East Kent buses; at the rear of the lower deck was a large luggage compartment. The bus was operated in London between BEA's terminal in Cromwell Road and Heathrow Airport, running alongside half-deck Regal IVs. It had a short life with BEA and by 1968 was running with Super Coaches of Upminster, with the lower saloon converted to a fully seated layout. It did, however, demonstrate the effectiveness of high-capacity double-deck buses on the airport service, although when these arrived in the mid-1960s they would be Routemasters rather than Regent Vs — a consequence of the BEA vehicles' being operated on the airline's behalf by London Transport.

In 1962 the Atomic Energy Research Establishment took 11 Regent Vs similar to the East Kent buses. These were used for staff transport at the AERE site at Harwell in Berkshire.

A rear-entrance version of the new Park Royal body was supplied to Mayne of Manchester on three 30ft Regent Vs in 1961 and on 10 on short-wheelbase chassis for Southampton City Transport in 1962. Southampton, with a fleet made up mainly of Guys, had ordered a dozen Leyland Titans in 1961, following that with a 20-vehicle order shared equally between Regent Vs and Titans. Southampton split its orders again in 1963 and then, from 1964, standardised on the Regent V, but with attractive bodywork by East Lancs or the associated Neepsend business. By the end of 1967 Southampton had 70 Regent Vs in its 180-strong fleet, but from 1968 it would standardise on the Leyland Atlantean. In 1966 the monthly magazine *Bus & Coach* road-tested a Southampton Regent V, fully laden and making four stops per mile, recording fuel consumption of 6.9mpg — which seems a poor figure when compared with Liverpool's reported 9.4mpg, or even the 8.77mpg which Halifax was getting from its Regent Vs, when in 1965 it published details of comparative trials of a range of types.

Right: While Leeds was buying conservative-looking open-platform buses Glasgow switched to forward entrances for its last Regent Vs — 89 buses with 72-seat Alexander bodywork, delivered between 1960 and 1962. They helped replace the city's last trams and arrived at the same time as 140 generally similar Leyland Titan PD3s. They represented AEC's last double-deck fleet order in Scotland. Stewart J. Brown

Left: Each year from 1960 to 1967 South Wales added Willowbrook-bodied Regent Vs to its fleet. This is a 1960 bus, a 30ft-long 71-seater. Geoffrey Morant

(At Halifax a Daimler CVG6LX was best, at 9.8mpg, a Guy Arab V demonstrator worst, at 8.32mpg.)

Cardiff Corporation was a new customer for the Regent V in 1961, taking 10 with 63-seat East Lancs bodies. More followed in 1962 and 1964, including some bodied in Sheffield by East Lancs' associate Neepsend but indistinguishable from the Blackburn-built products. Cardiff had previously bought six Bridgemasters and would later buy a batch of Swifts. It had 32 Regent Vs. The first 10 were 2D3RVs with vacuum brakes; the later deliveries were air-braked 2D3RAs.

Another new customer, but rather smaller, was Lowestoft Corporation. Lowestoft operated only 18 buses, and the two Massey-bodied Regent Vs delivered in 1963 were its first new buses since a pair of Regent IIIs in 1951. Subsequent new double-deckers for Lowestoft — there were just four more — would be Leyland Titans, but AECs reappeared in the fleet from 1969, when the Swift was adopted as the standard Lowestoft bus. In 1974 the Lowestoft bus operation became the responsibility of the new Waveney District Council, which took over the two Regent Vs (and the two Regent IIIs, by then 23 years old), although all four would be withdrawn the following year.

North of the border, AEC secured a few sales of Regent Vs with small operators in the 1960s. Garelochhead Coach Services, which had taken two Alexander-bodied MD-series chassis in 1958/9, switched to Northern Counties bodies in the 1960s — and to forward entrances. It stayed with the MD, however, taking one each year in 1964, 1965, 1966 and 1968. The first had a full-front body, never a common choice in Scotland, while the others were of conventional half-cab layout. The 1964 bus was also the last vacuum-braked Regent V to enter service, while that delivered in 1968 was the last Regent for a Scottish fleet and one of only three with a G-suffix registration (the other two being for Pontypridd Urban District Council); it also had the highest-numbered MD-series chassis, 2MD3RA645.

Members of the A1 co-operative in Ayrshire also bought Regent Vs in the first half of the 1960s. In 1963 came three with unusual Strachans bodywork (the only Regent Vs so bodied), and these were followed late in 1964 by two Massey-bodied buses — the last Regents to be bodied by that builder.

English independents buying Regent Vs in the first half of the 1960s included Mayne of Manchester, which, after taking three with Park Royal bodies in 1961, received two Neepsend-bodied 73-seaters in 1963 and three more in 1965, these bringing to 11 the number of Regent Vs Mayne was running on its service between Manchester city centre and Droylsden; subsequent double-deckers would be Daimler Fleetlines. Small operators in Yorkshire continued buying Regents with Roe bodies in the 1960s, Felix taking four and Blue Ensign and York Pullman one each. For the last two operators these were their second (and last) Regent Vs. And Barton Transport placed repeat orders for Regents with 30ft-long lowbridge Northern Counties bodies, but of forward-entrance layout. Forward-entrance lowbridge buses were very rare. The Barton buses — five in 1960 followed by six in 1963 — were particularly striking in having full-fronted bodies with curved windscreens on both decks. The body style was one of the most attractive built on a front-engined double-decker but was not specified by any other operator. The use of fixed curved-glass windscreens was made possible by a change in the Construction & Use Regulations which meant that there was no longer a requirement that the driver's windscreen on a bus or coach should have an opening section.

Following a large delivery of Regent Vs in 1960, Sheffield placed repeat orders, taking 10 with Weymann bodies in 1963, along with 17 with Park Royal bodies in 1963/4; all were forward-entrance 70-seaters. These were Sheffield's last Regents, and they would be followed by Swifts in 1968. Grimsby-Cleethorpes also took 30ft forward-entrance Regents at this time, seven Roe-bodied buses entering service in 1963/4. Douglas, which had

taken its first Regent Vs in 1957, started updating its fleet again in 1964 with three short 64-seaters bodied by Metro-Cammell — the operator's first forward-entrance double-deckers. They were followed in 1965 by two Willowbrook-bodied buses and in 1968 by two similar buses which were the last Regent Vs built, the final example having chassis number 3D2RA2024.

Below: The last Regent Vs for City of Oxford were two batches delivered in 1960. The first 10 had forward-entrance 63-seat East Lancs bodies. Here a brand-new bus stands alongside a Regent III with Northern Coachbuilders body in Oxford's Gloucester Green bus station. At this point the City of Oxford fleet was 100% AEC. Roy Marshall

Opposite page top: Later in 1960 came the final City of Oxford Regents, which were also the company's last lowbridge buses, as it then switched to lowheight Bridgemasters and Renowns. There were five buses in the batch, with bodies by East Lancs. The raised advertisement panel on the side was back-lit by fluorescent tubes, this being a concept that enjoyed brief popularity in the early 1960s. Omnicolour

Left: This Regent V 2D3RV
with Metro-Cammell
Orion body was one of 15
delivered to St Helens in
1961/2. St Helens then
temporarily abandoned AEC
as a supplier of double-
deckers, not taking any
more Regents until 1967,
when a further three similar
buses, but with air brakes,
were delivered. From 1954
St Helens prefixed its fleet
numbers with letters which
indicated — more or less —
the year in which the vehicle
was delivered; 'L' was used
for double-deckers received
in 1961, 1962 and 1965,
after which time the system
was dropped. Note the hub
cover on the rear wheel.
Omnicolour

Right: Bolton Corporation's only AEC Regents were six Mk Vs delivered in 1961, with 70-seat Metro-Cammell bodywork. The translucent panel behind the cab provided extra light on the staircase. These buses would pass to SELNEC PTE in 1969. Roy Marshall

Right: Only three Regent Vs were sold in Ireland, where Leyland's Titan ruled supreme with the country's state-owned transport operator, CIE. CIE built the body, the design of which could be traced back to Leyland bodies of the late 1930s. It had a certain style, even though the short bays meant there were six-and-a-half main side windows, at a time when the standard on a 30ft double-decker was five. The half-drop windows too were an anachronism and reflected the body's 1930s origins. The narrow entrance was located ahead of a large luggage compartment. CIE's livery at this time was two shades of green. These impressive buses were delivered in 1961 and replaced trains on the seven-mile line from Waterford to Tramore. The last would be withdrawn in 1976. Ian Allan Library

Above: **The last Regent Vs for Yorkshire Woollen District were 10 with 70-seat Northern Counties bodies in 1961. The only other Regent V to have 30ft-long forward-entrance Northern Counties bodywork of this style was a solitary vehicle for Hebble in 1962.**
Geoffrey Morant

Left: **Ten 30ft-long Regent Vs were delivered to Walsall in 1961, the order for 72-seat forward-entrance bodies divided equally between Willowbrook, as on this bus, and Metro-Cammell. Thin bands of yellow relief were enough to stop Walsall's all-over-blue livery looking drab. Walsall's Regent Vs would pass to West Midlands PTE in 1969.**
Roy Marshall

Right: Following the initial batch with full-front Park Royal bodies in 1958/9 all subsequent deliveries of Regent Vs to East Kent featured this more severe style of body, also by Park Royal. The first arrived in 1961, the last in 1967. A 1961 bus is seen in Margate in 1975, still in traditional East Kent livery but with corporate National Bus Company fleetname and advertising — and an NBC grey front wheel.
John Aldridge

Right: An unusual 1961 delivery was a solitary Regent V for British European Airways. The Park Royal body was of the same style as supplied that year to East Kent, but at the rear was a large luggage locker, complete with tail lift to aid loading. This bus would later be rebuilt with a conventional fully seated lower saloon and operated by Upminster & District. AEC

Above: Cardiff bought 32 Regent Vs, all with 63-seat bodywork by East Lancs or the associated Neepsend business. One of the 1961 deliveries is pictured on layover at the city's bus station. They cost £5,342 each. Stewart J. Brown

Below: Eastbourne Corporation took 22 Regent Vs with East Lancs bodies between 1956 and 1963. The upper-deck side windows were of the full-drop type, allowing summer visitors to enjoy the sea air, but could be locked shut by the conductor in bad weather. Here a 1961 bus loads outside the town's railway station in 1973 (below left), while a 1963 delivery (below right) shows the livery originally worn by most of Eastbourne's Regent Vs. Stewart J. Brown, Alan Snatt

Right: **Just three years separate this Huddersfield Regent V from that illustrated on page 41, but this 30ft-long bus with forward-entrance bodywork and new-look front is clearly a bus from the modern era. It was one of two delivered in 1961 and has East Lancs bodywork. Note the side destination display.**
Roy Marshall

Right: **Park Royal's double-deck output in the early 1960s could best be described as ungainly. The unequal-depth windows on each deck echoed the MCW group's Orion and Aurora bodies, and the short 'infill' window towards the rear of the upper deck on this 27ft-long body was peculiar, looking like an easy engineering solution rather than a carefully thought-out design feature. Southampton Corporation took 10 of these Park Royal-bodied Regent Vs in 1962 (along with similarly bodied Leyland Titan PD2s). The Corporation's later Regents would have rather more gently styled bodywork by East Lancs and Neepsend.**
Stewart J. Brown

Left: The only 30ft-long rear-entrance examples of the new Park Royal body were three supplied on Regent V chassis to Mayne of Manchester in 1961. They were 73-seaters. John Kaye

Below: Most of the Regent Vs delivered to Ipswich in the 1960s had bodywork by East Lancs or Neepsend. All were 65-seaters on 2D2RA chassis. This is one of three buses delivered in 1962 which were operated until 1977, when an influx of 15 new Leyland Atlanteans saw a like number of Regent Vs withdrawn. There is a period charm in the advertisement which reads: 'Sleep well on Sure-o-sleep mattresses and divans'. R. L. Wilson / Online Transport Archive

Above: Rhondda generally favoured short medium-weight Regent Vs, such as this 65-seat Metro-Cammell-bodied MD3RV, one of four delivered in 1962 and seen soon after entering service. Although broadly similar to that supplied by Weymann on 30ft-long buses delivered four years earlier — see page 44 — the bodywork shows detail differences, notably the absence of the inward curvature of the main lower-deck side panels and the use of deeper panels in place of fitting a separate guard rail. R. L. Wilson / Online Transport Archive

Right: The combination of Regent V chassis and Roe body was selected by a number of independents in Yorkshire, including Felix of Hatfield, which built up a fleet of eight. New in 1962, this was a 30ft-long 73-seater, seen in Doncaster at the Christchurch terminus used by the independents serving the town. Felix was bought by South Yorkshire PTE in 1976. Roger Holmes

Left: Devon General's last rear-entrance buses were seven Regent Vs delivered in 1962, with 59-seat Weymann Orion bodywork, one of which is seen passing Exeter bus station on a local service; in the background are assorted Royal Blue Bristols and an early Leyland Leopard/Plaxton Panorama of Black & White Motorways. Note also the Vauxhall Viva HA parked alongside a fine period piece in the shape of a concrete lamp-post. Omnicolour

Below: AEC's Regent V brochure for 1962 featured on the front a plan view of a long-wheelbase chassis. It described the Regent V somewhat vaguely as 'The world's leading double-deck bus chassis' — a claim with which Leyland might well have taken issue, at least in terms of sales volumes, for the contemporary Titan outsold the Regent V by a handsome margin. Ian Allan Library

REGENT
MARK V

The world's leading double deck bus chassis

Left: Sixteen of the 20 Regent Vs bought by Hebble were big-engined D-series models. The odd four MD-series chassis were delivered in 1962 and had 65-seat Northern Counties bodies. Here one of these handsome buses heads in to Bradford under the Corporation's trolleybus wires. Ian Allan Library

Right: **Bradford Corporation standardised on 30ft-long Regent Vs with forward-entrance Metro-Cammell bodywork seating 70. A total of 120 were delivered between 1959 and 1964, by which time they made up roughly one-third of the fleet. On this 1963 bus municipal pride is evident in the city's crest being displayed in the position normally occupied by the AEC badge, which has been relocated below the grille.** John Aldridge

Below: **Although by 1964, when this advertisement appeared in Bus & Coach, the MCW group was an established builder of bodies on rear-engined Atlanteans the bodybuilder chose a traditional bus — one of Bradford's Regent Vs — to promote the virtues of the 'lightweight, high-capacity double-decker'.** Gavin Booth collection

Right: **Strachans of Hamble built a small number of double-deckers in the 1960s. The only AECs to receive Strachans double-deck bodies were three Regent V 2D2RA models delivered to members of the A1 co-operative in 1963. Idiosyncratic features on the radiator grille are a star, which was not unusual on buses in Ayrshire, and the painting of vertical coloured stripes. The location is A1's bus station in Kilmarnock.** Harry Hay

Left: **Sheffield switched to forward-entrance bodywork for 31 Regent Vs delivered in 1963 and 1964.**
The 1963 buses included nine with Park Royal bodies. This 1973 view shows that light colours in industrial areas required a high level of body maintenance.
Stewart J. Brown

Below: **A Sheffield Regent V featured in this Park Royal advertisement, which appeared in *Bus & Coach* in December 1964.**
Gavin Booth collection

Left: **Lowestoft Corporation was one of the smallest municipal bus operators in England, running just 18 vehicles. In 1963 it purchased two medium-weight Regent Vs, with 61-seat Massey bodies. The use of the panel by the staircase for advertising — for a camera shop in the town —was unusual.**
Roy Marshall

Right: Very few front-engined double-deckers received bodywork with curved windscreens, and this feature certainly added a touch of modernity to 11 Regent Vs delivered to Barton Transport in the early 1960s. These buses were also unusual in being of forward-entrance lowbridge layout. One leaves Nottingham for Chilwell in 1974, pursued by an AEC Reliance coach that had been purchased to take advantage of the Government's New Bus Grant, which at this time met 50% of the cost of buying new one-man-operated vehicles.
'Bus grant' coaches would ultimately eliminate double-deckers from the Barton fleet. Stewart J. Brown

Right: Blue Ensign of Doncaster bought two Regent Vs, both with 71-seat forward-entrance Roe bodies. The newer of the two entered service in 1964 and is seen in 1973 departing from Doncaster's south bus station, one of two 1960s bus stations located under multi-storey car parks in the town. Nice touches are the chrome wheel trims and the use of the side advertising space to promote the company's private-hire business. The Regent Vs were withdrawn in 1975. Blue Ensign would be bought by South Yorkshire PTE in 1978.
Stewart J. Brown

Left: **York Pullman bought two Regent Vs with rear-entrance Roe bodies. The first was purchased in 1957, and the second, shown here, in 1964. Both were medium-weight models. In the mid-1960s York Pullman operated 20 buses and coaches, its fleet including four Regent IIIs as well as the two Regent Vs.**
Roy Marshall

Left: **Another buyer of Roe-bodied Regent Vs in 1964 was Grimsby-Cleethorpes Transport, which took three 70-seaters. They followed four similar buses delivered in 1963 and were the operator's last Regents.**
John Aldridge

Right: **Most of South Wales Transport's 1960s Regent Vs had Willowbrook bodies, but for the 20 delivered in 1964 the body order was shared between three suppliers — Willowbrook, Weymann and Park Royal. This is one of five Park Royal-bodied buses.**
The advertisement on the side warns that 'Passenger Transport Authorities would charge their losses to the rates' — part of a campaign of opposition by the BET group to the Government's plans in the 1960s to create PTAs in major urban areas.
Geoffrey Morant

Below: **Most Massey-bodied Regent Vs went to municipal operators, but the combination was also selected by three Scottish independents — Baxter's, Greenshields and A1. The last were two delivered to members of the A1 co-operative in 1964.**
Stewart J. Brown

Above: A unique style of full-fronted Northern Counties bodywork was fitted to this, the first forward-entrance double-decker for Garelochhead Coach Services. Full-fronted double-deckers were rare in Scotland, and this was one of just four new examples delivered to operators north of the border in the postwar period. It is seen outside Helensburgh station, the terminus of the company's service from Garelochhead. It was new in 1964.
Malcolm King

Left: From 1950 until 1967 all of Ipswich's motor buses were supplied by AEC, these including 44 Regent Vs delivered in the period 1957-66. The 1964 batch comprised just two vehicles, with 65-seat Massey bodies; other suppliers of bodywork on Regent Vs for Ipswich were Park Royal, East Lancs and Neepsend. Ipswich's Regents typically served the town for 17 years. Stewart J. Brown

# **Export boost**

**E**xports were important to AEC throughout the Regent V's production life. An initial order for 12 buses for the West Pakistan Road Transport Board in 1961 led to follow-on orders until 1967, taking the total to 118. The Kowloon Motor Bus Co in Hong Kong took 210 between 1963 and 1966, and the Regent V did well in the Middle East, deliveries to Teheran totalling 450 and to Baghdad 280 plus 28 spare chassis — 10% of the order. The KMB buses were big, with an extended 21ft 6in wheelbase and a bodied overall length of 34ft. To cope with the added weight and KMB's arduous operating territory the buses were fitted with the 154bhp 11.3-litre AV690 engine. The bodies were supplied in kit form by British Aluminium on the first 30 and Metal Sections on the remainder, for assembly in Hong Kong by KMB. They were dual-door 90-seaters, and typically gave KMB 21 years of service, the last being withdrawn in 1987. KMB would also buy second-hand Regent Vs in 1973/4, taking 28 forward-entrance buses, of which 21 had Metro-Cammell bodies and 22 had been new to BET fleets, including 15 ex-Rhondda buses. They typically ran for seven years with KMB, with new bodies and some re-powered with Gardner engines.

Closer to home, there were regular deliveries to Portugal. Early vehicles had Weymann bodies, but from 1960 AEC's Portuguese associate, UTIC, started building double-deck bodies for Lisbon, Oporto, Coimbra (two buses) and Guimaraes (just one bus), and then in 1964/5 produced complete integral vehicles using kits supplied by AEC. There were 57 such integrals, and externally they were indistinguishable from UTIC-bodied Regent V chassis. While Johannesburg was AEC's main Regent V buyer in Southern Africa, small batches of left-hand-drive Portuguese-style buses, 13 in all, were delivered to Luanda, the capital of the Portuguese colony of Angola. One Regent V chassis was shipped to Uruguay in 1963, its use there unknown.

The 2MD designation indicated a revised air-braking system on the medium-weight chassis and was first applied in 1963 to 10 Northern Counties-bodied buses for BET's Western Welsh subsidiary, which were followed in 1964 by 10 similar buses for Rhondda. At the same time sister BET company Devon General took the BET group's last vacuum-braked Regents, 16 Metro-Cammell-bodied buses delivered in 1963. By this stage all new Regents for BET were of forward-entrance layout, but orders from the

Right: The extra length of the Regent Vs for Kowloon Motor Bus is clearly illustrated in this view of a 1963 bus with a British Aluminium body which was assembled by KMB. KMB's Regents typically had a 21-year life. Alan Mortimer

group were slowing, as companies were switching to rear-engined Daimler Fleetlines and Leyland Atlanteans. Besides the 26 MD-series buses for Devon General and Western Welsh in 1963 there were 38 D-series deliveries for South Wales (25) and East Kent (13). The South Wales vehicles included a further six Roe-bodied single-deckers for Llanelli, which were Britain's last new half-cab single-deckers.

South Wales also bought low-height Renowns in 1963, and the company's General Manager, H. Weedy, writing in the *AEC Gazette* in 1962 noted: 'Whilst the [Regent] Mk V chassis has been most satisfactory in service, the new Renown has the edge by virtue of its low frame height and excellent suspension characteristics … The only factor which restricts its immediate adoption as a fleet chassis is the higher cost of the refinements which contribute to its superiority.' A polite way of saying the Renown was too expensive.

BET deliveries held up well in 1964, totalling 60, compared with 64 in the previous year. The 10 MD-series for Rhondda, mentioned above, were accompanied by 50 D-series models for Devon General (eight), Hebble (two), East Kent (20) and South Wales (20). Hebble's were its last

new Regents; the company would buy only one more new double-decker — a Daimler Fleetline in 1966. South Wales had in the late 1950s specified Weymann bodies, then from 1960 had standardised on Willowbrook bodywork. However, in 1964 its body order was split three ways between Weymann (nine), Willowbrook (six) and — a first for the fleet — Park Royal (five).

Lowbridge bodywork was not that common on Regent Vs, in part because AEC had alternative models on offer for operators that had problems with low bridges. BET companies had taken fewer than 50 lowbridge bodies on Regent V chassis before switching to Bridgemasters (or models from other manufacturers). The biggest user of lowbridge Regent Vs was City of Oxford, with 18. Independent operators took 21 lowbridge Regents, Barton Transport accounting for 13 of them, which were the only 30ft-long examples. And there were small numbers for municipal fleets — Newcastle, West Bridgford and Bedwas & Machen. The last lowbridge Regent was a Massey-bodied bus for Bedwas & Machen, in 1964. There were in total just 87 lowbridge Regent Vs.

Above: **Portugal was a significant market for AEC, 236 Regent V chassis being supplied in the period 1957-66, along with 57 kits which were assembled as integral vehicles by the company's associate in Portugal, UTIC. There was nothing to distinguish Southall-built Regent Vs from those constructed by UTIC. This is a mid-1960s UTIC-built model, seen in operation with Carris in Lisbon in 1979.** Stewart J. Brown

With 60 vehicles for BET and a few other large orders, including 30 for Bradford, 15 for Leeds and 12 for Cardiff, 1964 was the last year in which Regent deliveries would top the 100 mark. In 1965 they were down to 70, including 18 MD and 27 D models for BET companies. Unusually, Devon General took both types — six 59-seat Willowbrook-bodied MDs and six Park Royal 69-seat Ds. The medium-weight buses for Devon General were the last of their type for an English operator, although small numbers were still to be delivered to customers in Scotland and Wales.

The other main deliveries in 1965 were 10 buses for Leeds and part of a 15-vehicle order for Southampton. Deliveries to Southampton (20 buses) and East Kent (30) helped boost figures in 1966. This was the year Leeds took its last Regents. So too did BET's Welsh companies, South Wales Transport taking 18 Willowbrook-bodied buses, and Rhondda five medium-weight chassis with Northern Counties bodies. These took to 98 the number of Regent Vs in Rhondda service, out of a total fleet of 175 buses; indeed, at this point all of the company's double-deckers were Regents, there being a few Regent IIIs still in use. The last Regent V for an English independent was delivered to Felix of Hatfield in 1966 and was the company's eighth. Like most new double-deckers for Yorkshire independents it had a Roe body.

A new Welsh customer in 1965 was Pontypridd Urban District Council. The existing double-deckers in this 50-strong fleet were Bristol Ks and Guy Arabs, although AECs had been introduced to the operation in 1961 with the delivery of two Reliances. There were half a dozen Reliances in service when an order was placed for two Regent Vs with 60-seat Weymann bodies. These were Pontypridd's first forward-entrance double-deckers. Two which followed in 1966 had unusual forward-entrance Longwell Green bodies, the only bodies of this style produced by the small Bristol coachbuilder.

From the late 1950s Rotherham Corporation had divided its orders between Daimler and AEC, the latter supplying small numbers of Reliances, Bridgemasters and Renowns, and Daimler delivering CVG6/30 double-deckers. Thus there were eight AEC double-deckers — five Bridgemasters and three Renowns — in the fleet when Rotherham took its only Regents, three with forward-entrance Neepsend bodies, in 1966.

The 1966 Regents marked the final development of the model, with the use of the new 11.3-litre AV691 engine in place of the 9.6-litre AV590. The change was driven largely by the needs of truck operators seeking more power, although as installed in the Regent V the AV691 was rated at 128bhp, the same as the AV590. The new engine saw the chassis designation changed from 2D to 3D. Coming at a time when sales of rear-engined buses, double- and single-deck, were expanding rapidly, the 3D-series Regent V was to be a rare beast, just 50 being built for British operators. Most had Monocontrol transmission and were thus 3D2RA models (for Southampton, Rotherham and Douglas), but there were 15 manual-gearbox 3D3RA chassis for East Kent.

Devon General received its last Regents in 1966 — five 27ft-long 2D3RA models with 59-seat forward-entrance Metro-Cammell bodies. They took to 91 the number of Regent Vs in service with the company, of which 19 were heavy-duty D-series models.

The total number of Regent Vs delivered in 1967 was down to just 25. The year saw the last English Regent Vs entering service with three operators — East Kent, Southampton and St Helens. The 15 buses for East Kent brought to 161 the number of Regent Vs delivered to the company and to 767 the total bought by BET. They also had the last half-cab bodies built by Park Royal.

Southampton, which had first bought Regent Vs in 1962, now had a fleet of 70, its last 30 having AV691 engines, which made Southampton the biggest operator of the 3D-series chassis. The final 10, delivered in 1967, were the last double-deckers to be bodied by Neepsend. St Helens had been buying Regent Vs in the late 1950s and early 1960s, but the three delivered in 1967, which were AV590-powered 2D models, were its first for five years. They had rear-entrance Metro-Cammell Orion bodies and were the undertaking's last double-deckers. From 1968 St Helens would standardise on AEC Swifts.

Pontypridd's seven buses in 1967 marked that operator's biggest single order for new vehicles since nine Guys in 1957. The first bus took this small operator's fleet-number series to 99, and those that followed commenced a new series as 1-6.

Just three Regent Vs entered service in 1968 — two AV691-powered buses with Douglas Corporation and one with an AV470 engine with Garelochhead Coach Services. Then in 1969 two more Regents, this time with Willowbrook bodies, were delivered to Pontypridd and brought to an end the Regent story. These medium-weight models were the last new double-deckers for Pontypridd.

Left and below: From 1963 all of Devon General's Regent Vs were of forward-entrance layout. The company's 1965 deliveries comprised six 30ft-long 2D3RA models with 69-seat Park Royal bodies (left) and six short-wheelbase 2MD3RA models with 59-seat Willowbrook bodies (below). The Park Royal bodies were generally similar to those supplied to East Kent but with deeper skirt panels. Omnicolour, Stewart J. Brown collection

73

Right: The last Regents for Leeds City Transport were 20 with 70-seat Roe bodies, delivered in 1965/6. They brought its total of Regent Vs to 224 — roughly one-third of the fleet — and made Leeds the UK's biggest operator of the model. This is a 1973 view; note the advertisement promoting driver recruitment.
Stewart J. Brown

Right: Between 1956 and 1964 Bedwas & Machen purchased five Regent Vs, all medium-weight models with AV470 engines. This is the last, with 59-seat lowbridge Massey body, photographed in the operator's depot in March 1974 on the eve of local government reorganisation. It carries both its original fleet number (8) and the number (92) allocated in readiness for operation by Rhymney Valley District Council, which would take over the operation on 1 April. Stewart J. Brown

Left: In the mid-1960s
Southampton Corporation
standardised on the Regent
V with bodywork of this style
by East Lancs or the
associated Neepsend
company. This is a
Neepsend-bodied 66-seater
on a 2D3RA chassis, one of
15 delivered in 1964/5.
Stewart J. Brown

Below: Two Willowbrook-
bodied Regent Vs joined the
Douglas Corporation fleet in
1965, marking a change of
body supplier from Metro-
Cammell. They were 64-
seaters. Roy Marshall

Right: Since 1958 South Wales Transport had standardised on 30ft-long Regent Vs, but in 1965 the company switched to short models with 64-seat Willowbrook bodies. There were 21 that year, followed by a further 18 — the company's last Regents — in 1966/7, which brought to 108 the number of Willowbrook-bodied Regent Vs operated by SWT. R. L. Wilson / Online Transport Archive

Below: The last double-deckers to be built by Longwell Green of Bristol were supplied to Pontypridd in 1966. There were two of these Regent V 60-seaters, which had the only forward-entrance bodies produced by Longwell Green. They had 17-year operating lives, being withdrawn by Taff Ely, the successor to Pontypridd, in 1983. Omnicolour

Left: Rotherham Corporation was a latecomer to the Regent V. Three buses with 70-seat Neepsend bodies were delivered in 1966 and were examples of the comparatively rare 3D2RA model, with the AV691 engine. They followed earlier deliveries of Bridgemasters in 1960 and Renowns in 1964. The Regent Vs would pass to South Yorkshire PTE in 1974. Stewart J. Brown

Below: The medium-weight Regent V, by now in its 2MD3RA version, remained popular in Wales, being delivered in the mid-1960s to Pontypridd UDC and to BET subsidiary Rhondda. Pontypridd took seven with Metro-Cammell 60-seat bodies in 1967. Roy Marshall

Right: Scotland's last Regent V had the highest chassis number in the medium-weight series, 2MD3RA645. Actual production was 641, four numbers remaining unused. The last was for Garelochhead Coach Services, bringing to six the number of new Regent Vs in the fleet. It had a 64-seat Northern Counties body — among the last half-cab bodies produced by the Wigan-based coachbuilder. It entered service in November 1968 and is seen outside the operator's offices and depot in Garelochhead.
Stewart J. Brown

Right: The last heavy-duty D-series chassis were two for Douglas Corporation (chassis numbers 3D2RA2023/4) which entered service in 1968. They had AV691 engines, Monocontrol transmission and 64-seat Willowbrook bodywork. They took to 11 the number of Regent Vs in the Douglas fleet and were the operator's last new double-deckers. All 11 Regent Vs would pass in 1976 to the new Isle of Man National Transport company.
Omnicolour

Above: The last Regent Vs to enter service did so with Pontypridd in 1969. These were two 2MD3RA models with 60-seat Willowbrook bodies — the last half-cabs constructed by the Loughborough-based builder. The second of the pair is seen here when new, in March 1969. Note the AEC lettering on the grille. Roy Marshall

Left: When Regent V production ended some buyers turned to the AEC Swift. These included Ipswich, which took 11 in the early 1970s. The five delivered in 1973 had 40-seat dual-door East Lancs bodies. They were withdrawn in 1985 after 12 years — a rather shorter lifespan than the 17 years typically enjoyed by the operator's Regent Vs. Stewart J. Brown

# Regent retrospect

Given that double-deck buses of the 1950s and '60s were designed for a 15-year life, the oldest Regent Vs, dating from 1954, were still in service when the last were delivered in 1969. Consequently there were almost 2,300 Regent Vs in operation in Britain when the 1960s drew to a close. Indeed, there were still large numbers of Regent IIIs in service, although most of these were London Transport RTs.

But the move towards one-man operation, boosted in the 1970s by the availability of a 50% grant from the government towards the purchase of new buses to speed the replacement of conductors, meant that the Regent V — like other half-cab models — was in some fleets being replaced rather more rapidly than might otherwise have been the case. That said, Southampton's, for example, generally enjoyed a 14-year life, which was slightly better than the 12 years of the Atlanteans which

followed them, while many operators ran Regent Vs for longer. Interestingly, there is no evidence that the medium-weight models had notably shorter lives than did the heavyweights.

A few UK operators tried running half-cab double-deckers as one-man buses (albeit with little success), and East Kent adapted some of its Regent Vs. However, in South Africa Johannesburg tackled the issue by having one of its 1959 Regent Vs rebodied in 1977 with a full-front forward-entrance body by Bus Bodies. It wasn't a success; no more Johannesburg Regents were rebodied.

Changes to the bus-operating industry from the late 1960s saw the newly created Passenger Transport Executives acquiring Regent Vs from their constituent municipalities. All of the PTEs ran Regent Vs: Merseyside (from Liverpool and St Helens), SELNEC (Bolton and Rochdale), Tyne & Wear (Newcastle), West Midlands

Right: **This 1959 Regent V in the Johannesburg fleet was rebodied by Bus Bodies (South Africa) in 1977 for use as a one-man-operated vehicle. The body was generally similar to those fitted to Daimler Fleetlines around the same time. It is seen near the bodybuilder's Port Elizabeth factory, ready for the 1,000-kilometre delivery run to Johannesburg.** Rollo Dickson

Left: Although it looks like one of the 16 Regent Vs purchased by Halifax in 1960, this Weymann-bodied bus in Bradford is one of three former Hebble Regent Vs which joined the Halifax Joint Omnibus Committee fleet in March 1971 when it took over the bulk of Hebble's local bus services. In September of that year it passed to the new Calderdale JOC, which retained Halifax's distinctive livery. It would be taken over by West Yorkshire PTE in 1974. Geoffrey Morant

Below: For a short time in 1972/3 the Calderdale JOC operated four Park Royal-bodied Regent Vs, which it had purchased from Maidstone & District. Two were highbridge buses, as seen here, the other pair being lowbridge examples. Roy Marshall

Right: **In 1972 Gelligaer Urban District Council acquired a Park Royal-bodied Regent V from Western Welsh. The bus was 16 years old at the time of purchase and was operated for 12 months.** Roy Marshall

Below: **In 1973/4 Kowloon Motor Bus bought 28 second-hand Regent Vs from UK operators. Fifteen were former Rhondda buses, which were 12 years old. They were rebodied and served KMB until 1981/2.** Alan Mortimer

(Walsall), Greater Glasgow (Glasgow), West Yorkshire (Bradford, Leeds, Halifax and Huddersfield) and South Yorkshire (Sheffield, Rotherham, Doncaster). All would be gone by the end of the 1970s.

The National Bus Company inherited Regent Vs from a wide range of BET fleets — by coincidence all but one (Maidstone & District) were fleets which would adopt poppy red when NBC introduced its corporate livery in 1972. The biggest NBC Regent V fleets were at East Kent and South Wales Transport. The end of regular scheduled operation of Regents came at East Kent in 1981 and South Wales in 1982, although East Kent retained a few buses for school contracts until the middle of the decade.

BET companies accounted for precisely one-third of all home-market Regent V sales — 767 out of 2,285. And when it came to the medium-weight version of the chassis, BET's business accounted for not far short of half of sales — 307 of a total production of 641 (48%). Ten BET subsidiaries bought Regent Vs. BET did take more heavy-duty than medium-weight chassis, 460, although that was in part led by the move to 30ft-long buses. All but 46 of BET's D-series Regents were 30ft long.

But the Regent V's big success in the UK was with municipal operators, 31 (out of 97) between them buying 1,434 Regent Vs over the period 1957-69. Four of the biggest local authority fleets — Glasgow, Leeds, Liverpool and Sheffield — accounted for almost half of the sales to municipalities, taking 723 vehicles between them. Only two of the biggest

municipals — Birmingham and Manchester — did not buy Regent Vs.

Over the period of Regent V sales Leyland sold more than twice as many Titans to British operators — 5,555, against AEC's 2,285 Regents. Add Bridgemasters, Renowns and Routemasters to AEC's Regent V total, and AEC overtakes Leyland (albeit only just), taking AEC's total UK double-deck sales to 5,597. But — and it's a very big but — add Leyland's other double-deck models, the Atlantean and Lowlander, and you see that AEC was quite clearly no match for the Lancashire manufacturer. Between 1955 and 1969 Leyland delivered just over 12,500 double-deck buses to British operators, more than double the number supplied by AEC in the same period.

Looking at total Regent V sales, exports accounted for a major part, a total of 1,503 being delivered to eight countries — Angola, Hong Kong, Iran, Iraq, Portugal, South Africa, Uruguay and West Pakistan. Thus out of a total production of 3,788 vehicles, well over one third — 40% — were exported.

A total of 15 manufacturers built bodywork on the Regent V for home-market customers, ranging from small builders like Longwell Green, Reading and Strachans, on three chassis apiece, to the big names of the time, headed by Metro-Cammell and Weymann, with a combined total of 832. ACV's own bodybuilders, Park Royal, Roe and Crossley, bodied 824 Regent Vs. Crossley-bodied Regent Vs went to just two operators, Liverpool and Aberdeen.

The option of having a traditional exposed

Left: While all but a handful of the Regent Vs acquired by the National Bus Company were in fleets which would adopt the organisation's corporate poppy-red colour, they didn't necessarily remain red. A former East Kent vehicle is seen on driver-training duties with Maidstone & District in 1974 in NBC leaf green. Stewart J. Brown

Right: **More typical of East Kent's Regent Vs in NBC days is this 1959 bus, seen in Margate in the mid-1970s. It is smartly turned out, in the East Kent tradition, but NBC's poppy red was no substitute for the company's previous livery of maroon and cream.**
John Aldridge

radiator was taken up by just a few Regent V buyers, and mostly on medium-weight chassis, 251 of which were so fitted, along with 52 D-series models, making a total of 303. More than half of these, 164, were for one operator, Leeds City Transport.

Hindsight is a wonderful thing, and looking back at some of the decisions taken by AEC some 50 years ago it's possible to see the seeds of the company's weakening position as a supplier of double-deck buses. Developing the low-height Bridgemaster was a reasonable decision, although developing it as an integral was perhaps less sensible, however appealing the idea of selling complete buses might have been to ACV's management. While AEC was designing the Bridgemaster Leyland was already publicly experimenting with new rear-engined prototypes, but it has to be remembered that the early vehicles were complex and expensively engineered, and there was in the mid-1950s no guarantee that the bus industry would embrace the concept of a rear-engined double-decker.

Similarly the work done by ACV in developing the Routemaster must have seemed sensible at the time. AEC had been London's principal supplier of buses since the creation of London Transport (and before), and it is understandable that winning continuing orders from LT was considered a prize worth pursuing — even more so when the order was for complete ACV-sourced vehicles, with AEC running units and Park Royal bodywork.

Yet from 1958 Leyland was winning new orders in large numbers for its revolutionary Atlantean. By the end of 1960 there were in service almost 650 Atlanteans, and Daimler had announced it was building an Atlantean competitor, the Fleetline. And what was AEC's response? The front-engined Renown. The first Renowns entered service in 1963, by which time there were some 1,300 rear-engined double-deckers in operation in the UK. That AEC was out of step with the march of progress was perhaps most clearly illustrated by comparative trials conducted in 1965 by Edinburgh Corporation, as it sought to plan its future bus-purchasing policy. The three main manufacturers each provided Edinburgh with a demonstrator — Daimler a Fleetline, Leyland an Atlantean, and AEC a Renown. That AEC had last supplied new buses to Edinburgh in 1951 was immaterial. The Renown was by then quite clearly the bus of the past; the Atlantean and Fleetline were the models of the future.

So it is possible to argue that AEC's efforts in developing the Routemaster and two low-height models diverted its attention from the changes taking place in the bus industry and in particular the growing acceptance of rear-engined models. And its development of a rear-engined version of the integral Routemaster ignored the fact that a large number of bus operators liked to have the freedom to choose their own bodybuilders.

When Bristol was developing its rear-engined VR there were plans to offer it with an AEC AV691 engine (as a VRTSL6A?), which would have allowed Regent customers to buy an AEC-engined double-decker. But the idea came to nought, attractive as it might have sounded to buyers of the Regent V.

There had, of course, been a significant change at ACV in May 1962, when it was merged with Leyland Motors. That had no immediate impact on AEC's bus range, including the Regent, which continued to compete for business with the Leyland Titan, but it probably did influence the future of the rear-engined Routemaster, which, in fact, had no future.

The end of the Regent after 40 years in various guises did not mark the end of AEC as a supplier of urban buses. The rear-engined Swift was bought by a number of operators which had previously bought Regent Vs, among them 16 municipalities — Aberdeen, Bradford, Cardiff, Great Yarmouth, Grimsby-Cleethorpes, Huddersfield, Ipswich, Leeds, Lowestoft, Morecambe & Heysham, Nottingham, Rochdale, St Helens, Sheffield, Southampton and West Bridgford. Three Regent V-operating BET companies, City of Oxford, East Kent and South Wales, also bought Swifts, as did one independent, York Pullman. The Swift also attracted new customers to AEC, such as Belfast and Sunderland corporations.

However, Swift production came to an end in 1975, the last examples for the UK entering service with Grimsby-Cleethorpes in December, and that really did mark the end of AEC as a supplier of purpose-built urban buses — although a few independents continued to specify bus bodies on mid-engined Reliance chassis right up to the end of the decade. The Swift had been a victim of Leyland's focus on the integral National, which saw BL axe the competing single-deck chassis in its range.

The AEC company itself would ultimately become a victim of BL rationalisation. When production of the Swift came to an end the company continued building Reliances and front-engined Rangers for export. It was also supplying kits for overseas assembly, most notably for UTIC integral coaches in Portugal and for the rugged front-engined Kudu in South Africa. Right to the end, Rangers and Kudus were supplied with Regent V-style grilles.

The end for AEC came in 1979, when the factory at Windmill Lane in Southall closed, after just over 50 years producing lorries and bus chassis, including around 20,000 Regents — no mean achievement.

Left: **Another smart livery to disappear with the introduction of NBC's corporate identity was that used by Devon General. By now in NBC red, a 1964 Willowbrook-bodied bus heads into Exeter bus station in 1978.** Mark Bailey

85

Left: BET's last medium-weight Regent Vs were five Northern Counties-bodied examples which entered service with Rhondda in 1965. They were 65-seaters. This one is seen in Merthyr Tydfil in 1974, in NBC poppy red and in the ownership of Western Welsh, which had absorbed the Rhondda business in 1970. Stewart J. Brown

Below: Regent Vs were popular second-hand purchases, many finding second lives with independent operators after withdrawal by their original owner. In 1971 Charlton on Otmoor Services was running this former South Wales Transport bus, seen in Oxford. New in 1954, it had a Weymann Orion body. John Aldridge

Left: **Suffolk operator Norfolk's** owned this former Bolton Corporation Regent, acquired from SELNEC PTE and pictured heading out of Colchester bus station for its home village of Stoke-by-Nayland in 1977. New in 1961, it had a Metro-Cammell body. Note the sliding entrance door; most operators of forward-entrance double-deckers specified double jack-knife doors. Stewart J. Brown

Above: **In less than 10 years between the mid-1960s and the mid-1970s Barton Transport was transformed from a remarkably varied fleet into one running only bus-grant coaches. Its double-deckers were sold, and by 1976 Redfern, of Mansfield, was running this ex-Barton Regent V — one of four acquired, primarily for school services.** John Aldridge

Above: **This former East Kent Regent V was one of a number converted to open-top and is seen in service with National Travel South East in 1977. Normally white, it had been repainted silver to celebrate HM The Queen's Silver Jubilee. This bus was new in 1959 and had a Park Royal body.** Stewart J. Brown

Right: Most of the AEC Regent Vs operated by SELNEC PTE were acquired from Rochdale Corporation. A 1956 bus is seen in 1973 in SELNEC's distinctive livery, with Northern Division fleetname. Note the SELNEC advertisement on the side. John Robinson

Below: Merseyside PTE acquired 186 Regent Vs from Liverpool Corporation. The PTE initially retained the Corporation's livery for its Liverpool division — this avoided having to repaint the fleet — so only the logo above the driver's cab reveals this Regent to be in PTE ownership. A 1958 bus with Metro-Cammell body, it was photographed in Liverpool city centre in 1973. Stewart J. Brown

Left: **In 1974 the Merseyside PTE area was expanded to include Southport and St Helens. Here a Metro-Cammell-bodied Regent V of 1962 stands outside the St Helens Corporation depot in May 1974, displaying its new owner's logo in place of the town's coat of arms.** Stewart J. Brown

Above: **West Yorkshire PTE took over AEC Regents from all of its municipal constituents. An ex-Bradford bus is seen in Bradford city centre in 1976. It was new in 1963 and, like all Bradford's Regent Vs, had 70-seat Metro-Cammell bodywork.** Stewart J. Brown

Above: **South Yorkshire PTE acquired 63 Regent Vs from Sheffield. They included this 1960 Alexander-bodied bus, seen in Sheffield city centre in 1976, two years after the formation of the PTE but with no obvious signs of the change of ownership.** Stewart J. Brown

Above: One former Sheffield Alexander-bodied Regent V ended its days with a South Yorkshire independent, Premier of Stainforth. It is seen in Doncaster.
Roy Marshall

Right: Local-government reorganisation in 1974 saw the merger of a number of municipal fleets in England and Wales. The new Rhymney Valley District Council operation combined the Gelligaer, Caerphilly and Bedwas & Machen fleets, the last-named contributing three Regent Vs. This was the newest, a 1964 Massey-bodied 2MD3RA, seen on an enthusiasts' tour in 1979; the last Regent V to be fitted with lowbridge bodywork, it would be withdrawn later that year.
Stewart J. Brown

Above: **In 1974, as part of the changes brought about by local-government reorganisation, Waveney District Council took over the 20 buses operated by Lowestoft Corporation. On 3 December 1977 Waveney ceased bus operation, the services being taken over by Eastern Counties, and the buses, which included this 1963 Massey-bodied Regent V, sold.** Roy Marshall

Left: **With Bristol VRTs in the background, a late Regent survivor in the Cardiff fleet turns in to the city's bus station in 1979. Orange had replaced maroon as the Cardiff livery in 1972. At the same time the use of both Welsh and English was adopted for the fleetname, with a different language on each side of the bus — a novel idea in the 1970s. New in 1964, this bus had an East Lancs body.** Stewart J. Brown

91

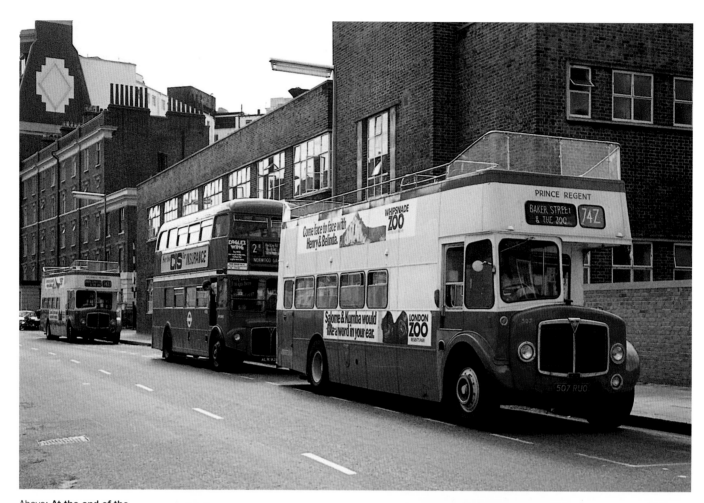

Above: **At the end of the 1970s two 1964 Willowbrook-bodied Regent Vs which had been converted to open-top joined the Obsolete Fleet operation in London, being used primarily on the 74Z route, which ran from Baker Street Tube station to London Zoo. Initially they retained NBC poppy red and white — they had been part of the Devon General fleet — although one would later be repainted in London red. Both buses are seen here on layover in Baker Street, sandwiching a Routemaster. They were named** Prince Regent **and** Regency Princess. John Aldridge

Right: **At the start of the 1980s there were still 13 Regent Vs in service with Ipswich Corporation. This 1966 Neepsend-bodied bus — pictured in the town's bus station in 1983 — was a late survivor, remaining in service until 1986.** Stewart J. Brown

Left: Regent Vs served Lisbon until the mid-1980s, by which time they were being replaced by conventional European single-deck city buses. This 1985 photograph shows the brighter livery which from the late 1970s had replaced the original green. Stewart J. Brown

Below: The heyday of Devon General is captured in this photograph taken in Plymouth in 2009 at the annual rally organised by the Western National Preservation Group. In the lead is a 1965 2MD3RA with Willowbrook body, a 1956 Metro-Cammell-bodied MD3RV following. Mark Bailey

93

Right: One survivor has been saved from the biggest UK order for Regent Vs — that placed by Glasgow Corporation for 89 Alexander-bodied buses to help replace the city's trams in the early 1960s. The restored bus, housed in the Glasgow Vintage Vehicle Trust's museum, wears an anachronistic livery; this attractive colour scheme was superseded in 1959 by a simpler combination of yellow and green (as shown on page 52), and none of the Corporation's forward-entrance Regent Vs operated in this livery.
Stewart J. Brown

Below: This Regent V from the Oporto fleet has been preserved in Portugal. Oporto had 10 such buses with 67-seat UTIC bodies, new in 1960. From 1962 Oporto bought Atlanteans.
Gavin Booth

# Appendices

## 1: REGENT V OPERATORS

### British Isles

#### Municipal / JOC

| | MD series | D series | Total |
|---|---|---|---|
| Aberdeen Corporation | 30 | - | 30 |
| Bedwas & Machen UDC | 5 | - | 5 |
| Bolton Transport | - | 6 | 6 |
| Bradford City Transport | - | 120 | 120 |
| City of Cardiff Transport | - | 32 | 32 |
| Colchester Corporation | - | 11 | 11 |
| Darwen Corporation | - | 1 | 1 |
| Doncaster Corporation | 31 | - | 31 |
| Douglas Corporation | - | 11 | 11 |
| Eastbourne Corporation | - | 22 | 22 |
| Glasgow Corporation | - | 164 | 164 |
| Great Yarmouth Corporation | 13 | - | 13 |
| Grimsby-Cleethorpes | 7 | 7 | 14 |
| Halifax Corporation/JOC | - | 16 | 16 |
| Hartlepool Corporation | 4 | - | 4 |
| Huddersfield JOC | - | 18 | 18 |
| Ipswich Corporation | - | 44 | 44 |
| Leeds City Transport | 150 | 74 | 224 |
| Liverpool Corporation | - | 193 | 193 |
| Lowestoft Corporation | 2 | - | 2 |
| Morecambe & Heysham | 5 | - | 5 |
| Newcastle Transport | 40 | - | 40 |
| Nottingham City Transport | - | 65 | 65 |
| Pontypridd UDC | 13 | - | 13 |
| Rochdale Corporation | - | 55 | 55 |
| Rotherham Corporation | - | 3 | 3 |
| Sheffield Transport | - | 142 | 142 |
| Southampton City Transport | - | 70 | 70 |
| St Helens Corporation | 14 | 43 | 57 |
| Walsall Corporation | 1 | 10 | 11 |
| West Bridgford UDC | 6 | 6 | 12 |
| **Total municipal** | **321** | **1,113** | **1,434** |

#### BET

| | MD series | D series | Total |
|---|---|---|---|
| City of Oxford | 48 | 16 | 64 |
| Devon General | 72 | 19 | 91 |
| East Kent | - | 161 | 161 |
| East Yorkshire | 17 | 2 | 19 |
| Hebble | 4 | 16 | 20 |
| Maidstone & District | 22 | - | 22 |
| Rhondda | 58 | 40 | 98 |
| South Wales | 61 | 153 | 214 |
| Western Welsh | 25 | 9 | 34 |
| Yorkshire Woollen | - | 44 | 44 |
| **Total BET** | **307** | **460** | **767** |

#### Independent

| | MD series | D series | Total |
|---|---|---|---|
| A1 Service, Ardrossan | - | 5 | 5 |
| Barton, Chilwell | - | 13 | 13 |
| Baxter, Airdrie | 2 | - | 2 |
| Bingley, Kinsley | - | 2 | 2 |
| Blue Ensign, Doncaster | - | 2 | 2 |
| Burrows, Wombwell | 1 | - | 1 |
| Cottrell, Mitcheldean | 1 | 1 | 2 |
| Felix, Hatfield | - | 8 | 8 |
| Garelochhead Coach Services | 6 | - | 6 |
| Greenshields, Salsburgh | 1 | - | 1 |
| Kearsey, Cheltenham | 1 | - | 1 |
| Samuel Ledgard, Leeds | - | 6 | 6 |
| A. Mayne & Son, Manchester | - | 11 | 11 |
| Osborne, Tollesbury | - | 1 | 1 |
| York Pullman | 2 | - | 2 |
| **Total independent** | **14** | **49** | **63** |

#### Other

| | MD series | D series | Total |
|---|---|---|---|
| AEC (demonstrators) | 2 | - | 2 |
| AERE, Harwell | - | 11 | 11 |
| BEA, London | - | 1 | 1 |
| CIE | - | 3 | 3 |
| Coal Industry Welfare | 1 | - | 1 |
| Leeds City Welfare | 1 | - | 1 |
| Pilkington, St Helens (vans) | - | 2 | 2 |
| **Total other** | **4** | **17** | **21** |
| **Total home-market sales** | **646** | **1,639** | **2,285** |

### EXPORT

| | MD series | D series | Total |
|---|---|---|---|
| Baghdad, Iraq* | - | 308 | 308 |
| Coimbra, Portugal | - | 2 | 2 |
| Guimaraes, Portugal | - | 1 | 1 |
| Johannesburg, South Africa | - | 110 | 110 |
| Kowloon Motor Bus, | - | 210 | 210 |
| Lisbon, Portugal | - | 223 | 223 |
| Luanda, Angola | - | 13 | 13 |
| Oporto, Portugal | - | 10 | 10 |
| Uruguay | - | 1 | 1 |
| Teheran, Iran | - | 450 | 450 |
| UTIC kits, Portugal | - | 57 | 57 |
| West Pakistan | - | 118 | 118 |
| **Total export sales** | **-** | **1,503** | **1,503** |
| **GRAND TOTAL** | **646** | **3,142** | **3,788** |

* including 28 chassis for spares

## 2: TOP 10 UK REGENT V BUYERS

| | |
|---|---|
| Leeds City Transport | 224 |
| South Wales | 214 |
| Liverpool Corporation | 193 |
| Glasgow Corporation | 164 |
| East Kent | 161 |
| Sheffield Transport | 142 |
| Bradford City Transport | 120 |
| Rhondda | 98 |
| Devon General | 91 |
| Southampton City Transport | 70 |

Eight of the top 10 Regent V buyers had previously bought Regent IIIs. Only East Kent and Southampton were new customers for AEC double-deckers, although East Kent was already operating significant numbers of Reliances.

## 3: EXPOSED-RADIATOR REGENT Vs

| | MD series | D series | Total |
|---|---|---|---|
| Bedwas & Machen UDC | 1 | - | 1 |
| City of Oxford | 33 | - | 33 |
| Doncaster Corporation | 31 | - | 31 |
| East Yorkshire | 17 | - | 17 |
| Huddersfield JOC | - | 8 | 8 |
| Leeds City Transport | 150 | 14 | 164 |
| Nottingham City Transport | - | 30 | 30 |
| Rhondda | 19 | - | 19 |
| **Total** | **251** | **52** | **303** |

## 4: BODYBUILDERS FOR HOME-MARKET DOUBLE-DECK REGENT Vs

| | Highbridge | Lowbridge | Total |
|---|---|---|---|
| Alexander | 166 | - | 166 |
| CIE | 3 | - | 3 |
| Crossley | 72 | - | 72 |
| East Lancs / Neepsend | 172 | 5 | 177 |
| Longwell Green | 2 | 1 | 3 |
| Massey | 35 | 7 | 42 |
| Metro-Cammell | 457 | - | 457 |
| Northern Counties | 56 | 13 | 69 |
| Park Royal | 397 | 31 | 428 |
| Reading | - | 3 | 3 |
| Roe | 311 | 3 | 314 |
| Strachans | 3 | - | 3 |
| Weymann | 353 | 22 | 375 |
| Willowbrook | 159 | 2 | 161 |
| **Total** | **2,186** | **87** | **2,273** |

## 5: REGENT V CHASSIS CODES

**16ft 4in wheelbase, AV470 engine**
MD2RA Medium weight, Monocontrol gearbox, air brakes (Aberdeen and Leeds only)
MD3RV Medium weight, synchromesh gearbox, vacuum brakes
2MD3RA Series 2, medium weight, synchromesh gearbox, split-system air brakes

There was no medium-weight model with the combination of Monocontrol transmission and vacuum brakes, which would have been coded MD2RV.

**16ft 4in or 18ft 7in (from 1959) wheelbase, A218, AV590 or AV691 engine**
D2RA A218 engine, Monocontrol gearbox, air brakes
D2RV A218 engine, Monocontrol gearbox, vacuum brakes
D3RV A218 engine, synchromesh gearbox, vacuum brakes
2D2RA AV590 engine, Monocontrol gearbox, air brakes
2D3RA AV590 engine, synchromesh gearbox, air brakes
2D3RV AV590 engine, synchromesh gearbox, vacuum brakes
3D2RA AV691 engine, Monocontrol gearbox, air brakes
3D3RA AV691 engine, synchromesh gearbox, air brakes (East Kent only)

**16ft 4in wheelbase, Gardner 6LW engine**
D2RA6G Monocontrol or preselector gearbox, air brakes (Rochdale only)
D2RV6G Preselector gearbox, vacuum brakes (Glasgow and Aberdeen only)

**18ft 7in wheelbase, A218 or AV590 engine**
LD2RA Monocontrol gearbox, air brakes
LD3RA Synchromesh gearbox, air brakes
2LD3RA Series 2, synchromesh gearbox, air brakes

There were no long-wheelbase chassis with vacuum brakes. The L codes were dropped in 1959, 30ft-long chassis thereafter having the same code as the short-wheelbase models with AV590 or AV691 engines.

All export chassis had air brakes and generally used the same codes as home-market models, left-hand-drive models being coded D2LA or LD2LA.